More Hollywood Homes

Mike Oldham

Schiffer Publishing Ltd

4880 Lower Valley Road, Atglen, Pennsylvania 19310

Dedication

To Judy Artunian, who co-started the string of Hollywood book projects.

Schiffer Books are available at special discounts for bulk purchases for sales promotions or premiums. Special editions, including personalized covers, corporate imprints, and excerpts can be created in large quantities for special needs. For more information contact the publisher:

Published by Schiffer Publishing Ltd.
4880 Lower Valley Road
Atglen, PA 19310
Phone: (610) 593-1777; Fax: (610) 593-2002
E-mail: Info@schifferbooks.com

For the largest selection of fine reference books on this and related subjects, please visit our web site at
www.schifferbooks.com
We are always looking for people to write books on new and related subjects. If you have an idea for a book please contact us at the above address.

This book may be purchased from the publisher.
Include $3.95 for shipping.
Please try your bookstore first.
You may write for a free catalog.

In Europe, Schiffer books are distributed by
Bushwood Books
6 Marksbury Ave.
Kew Gardens
Surrey TW9 4JF England
Phone: 44 (0) 20 8392-8585; Fax: 44 (0) 20 8392-9876
E-mail: info@bushwoodbooks.co.uk
Website: www.bushwoodbooks.co.uk

Other Schiffer Books by Mike Oldham
Greetings from Beverly Hills

Other Schiffer Books on Related Subjects
Architecture Tours L.A.: Guidebook Hollywood. Laura Massino Smith.
Architecture Tours L.A.: Guidebook West Hollywood/Beverly Hills. Laura Massino Smith.
Hollywood Collectibles. Dian Zillner.
Hollywood Collectibles: The Sequel. Dian Zillner.
Hollywood Homes Postcard Views of Early Stars' Estates. Mary L. Martin, Tina Skinner, & Tammy Ward.
Hollywood Movie Posters: 1914-1990. Miles Barton.
Hollywood Movie Songs Collectible Sheet Music. Marion Short.
Stars of the New Jersey Shore: A Theatrical History. Karen Schnitzspahn.

Copyright © 2008 by Mike Oldham
Library of Congress Control Number: 2007938801

Designed by Mark David Bowyer
Type set in Bernhard Modern BT / Humanist 521 BT

ISBN: 978-0-7643-2902-9
Printed in China

Contents

Acknowledgments

Tina Skinner, of Schiffer Publishing, chatted with me about this book project in Pasadena, California. That conversation got the ball rolling toward publication. I thank her for that. Tina has no ego whatsoever, and that is refreshing in the book publishing business!

I took comfort knowing Jeff Snyder of Schiffer Publishing looked at the book prior to its printing. He's an editor that doesn't mind pestering questions!

I would like to thank Judy Artunian for proofreading this manuscript. Yes, she was paid for this job and for working on my previous book on Beverly Hills. But I always suspect Judy takes such assignments because she just cannot resist any project involving silent stars! I really cannot imagine doing a book without her involvement. A bonus in hiring Judy is getting some of her Hollywood knowledge. Who else would suggest that I drop in a line or two about actress Aileen Pringle being a friend of actor Rudolph Valentino? Only Judy!

A debt of gratitude from me goes out to the silent stars of Hollywood. In doing the research on silent stars I have come to realize that these actors and actresses have been rather historically shy. A lot of their biographical information remains, well, silently hidden from the public. To get at it, you really have to want it. That is what makes the silent stars fascinating to research. For remaining mysterious, I thank the silent stars.

Finally, I would like to thank all the silent-star family members of mine who got their start in the talkies.

Introduction

A couple of years ago I won a bid on eBay for a postcard that featured silent-star Aileen Pringle's home in Santa Monica, California. It would be another postcard to add to my growing movie star home postcard collection. The card arrived in the mail a few days later. The address of Pringle's home was printed on the front of the card: 722 Adelaide, Santa Monica, California. I must have been walking by it all these years! I flipped the card over and read a sentence printed on the back, "A castle within the shadows of Hollywood's famous homes." I did not know much about Pringle, but my curiosity about the silent-film actress was growing. My thinking was that Pringle was not only a silent star, but also a famous one. Otherwise, why else would someone bother making a postcard of her home? But before I investigated Pringle, I had to find her house.

I parked my car on San Vicente Boulevard, walked a half block to Seventh Street, and made a right. Within a minute or so, I made another right on Adelaide Place. My heart started to pound. Would the house be there? Would it look the same as the postcard view from decades ago? Suddenly, I glanced right and there was Pringle's house! It matched the postcard picture. Gazing at the house, I stood in the street in a state of reverie.

While standing in front of the home it occurred to me that I might just be the only person in the last seven or eight decades to come here just to view Pringle's house … and to enjoy it for what it still is, a movie star's home. I pictured Pringle walking through the front door. Could she have imagined someone in the twenty-first century driving sixty miles to see her home?

I drove home, making a mental note to research Pringle further. Questions were running through my mind: "Was she in films with Valentino, Fairbanks, Gish, or Gilbert? When did she die? Was she rich or poor? Was she forgotten or revered after retiring?"

That experience is what *More Hollywood Homes* is all about.

— Mike Oldham

"Housekeeping" Notes

More Hollywood Homes is meant as a companion to *Hollywood Homes: Postcard Views of Early Stars' Estates* (Schiffer Publishing Ltd., 2005). Therefore, this book offers postcard homes/views not found in *Hollywood Homes* and vice versa.

All of the homes in this book are postcard views. However, not all of the images of the stars in this book were postcards. Some of the postcard views were part of a postcard packet foldout and are indicated as such.

Postcards have been known to contain factual errors and misspellings. Some cards place the location of a house in the wrong city. The postcard of the Bel-Air home of actress Colleen Moore incorrectly puts its location in Beverly Hills. Other errors involve the stars themselves that are listed as living in a given house. The card depicting the postcard home of actor Douglas Fairbanks, Jr. incorrectly labels the home as belonging to both Fairbanks, Jr. and actress Joan Crawford. There are postcards—very few in number—that have incorrectly placed a star as living in a home where he/she never actually took up residence. I did not place card corrections notes in the manuscript for a number of reasons. The only exception being the Fairbanks, Jr. and Joan Crawford card where I point out that Joan Crawford never lived at the house.

The Stars and Their Homes

Julie Andrews (1935–)

Actress

Memorable Films: *Mary Poppins* (1964); *The Sound of Music* (1965).

Although it has been decades since she starred in *Mary Poppins* (1964) and *The Sound of Music* (1965), actress Julie Andrews is still strongly identified with those films. Among her later film successes are *Victor Victoria* (1982) and *The Princess Diaries* (2001). Andrews has been married to director Blake Edwards since the late 1960s.

Richard Arlen (1898–1976) and Jobyna Ralston (1899–1967).

Actor (Arlen) and Actress (Ralston)

Memorable Films (Richard Arlen): *Wings* (1927); *Grand Canyon* (1949).

Memorable Films (Jobyna Ralston): *The Kid Brothers* (1927); *Wings* (1927).

Born in Virginia, Richard Arlen began his acting career in the early 1920s with uncredited parts. It can be said he crash-landed into films. While working at Marathon Street Studio as a messenger boy, he crash-landed the delivery motorcycle and broke a leg. According to screenwriter Jesse Lasky Jr., the studio offered Arlen a movie part in hopes of discouraging him from suing the studio. "It is probable Richard Arlen wouldn't have sued anyway," said Lasky, Jr. "In his parts, and in his life, Arlen was always the perfect gentleman." Arlen married actress Jobyna Ralston in the late 1920s. Ralston's film career began in the early 1920s and is not memorable.

Arlen was among the first movie stars to move into the Los Angeles community of Toluca Lake. He shared this distinction with the likes of actors W.C. Fields and Mary Astor. Arlen shared a home in the area with Ralston.

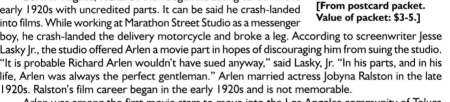

Home of Julie Andrews.
[From postcard packet. Value of packet: $3-5.]

Richard Arlen

Home of Richard Arlen and Jobyna Ralston. [Value of card: $3-5.]

Fred Astaire (1899–1987).

Actor

Memorable Films: *Top Hat* (1935); *Swing Time* (1936).

It's hard to think of dancer and actor Fred Astaire without thinking of his co-star, Ginger Rogers. And it's no wonder. After the two made the 1933 film, *Flying Down to Rio*, they danced together to stardom. In the mid-1930s, RKO Radio Pictures offered Astaire ten percent of the profits for all his films.

Astaire's wife, Phyllis, was responsible for building their dream house in the late 1930s. In addition to finding the Beverly Hills property, "she was engrossed in plans and blueprints for building operations which were to start almost immediately," recalled the actor.

"Fred [Astaire] was a hard taskmaster, a perfectionist. He always got a little cross with me because my concentration was not as dedicated to the projects as his was. So there were times of stress."

—Actress Ginger Rogers

Fred Astaire

Fred Astaire

Home of Fred Astaire. [Value of card: $8-10.]

8

Lucille Ball (1911–1989)

Actress

Memorable Television Show: "I Love Lucy" (1951–1957).

Actress Lucille Ball appeared in movies, but people under a certain age, who identify Ball only with her role as Lucy Ricardo on the 1950s sitcom "I Love Lucy," might find that hard to believe. The show co-starred her husband, Desi Arnaz, and was produced by their company, Desilu Productions.

Ultimately, Ball and Arnaz did not have a marriage made for television. They divorced in 1960. "I think they were the happiest when they were working together on 'I Love Lucy' or dealing with business at Desilu," recalled daughter Lucie Arnaz.

Home of Lucille Ball.
[Value of card: $3-5.]

Home of Lucille Ball. [From postcard packet. Value of packet: $3-5.]

George Bancroft (1882–1956).

Actor

Memorable Films: *Underworld* (1927); *Mr. Deeds Goes to Town* (1936).

The 1925 film *Code of the West* was an upward turning point for George Bancroft. He became a tough-guy star in the late 1920s and in later years he was a stalwart character actor.

Bancroft owned an oceanfront home in Santa Monica for many years. He moved into the home in the 1920s.

George Bancroft

GEORGE BANCROFT'S HOME, 978 OCEAN FRONT DRIVE, SANTA MONICA, CALIFORNIA

Home of George Bancroft. [Value of card: $3-5.]

Gene Barry (1919–)

Actor

Memorable Television Show: "Burke's Law" (1963–1966).

Actor Gene Barry won a Golden Globe for his work on the television series "Burke's Law." As a kid, he could play the violin so well he was considered a virtuoso. In the 1990s, Barry starred in a new "Burke's Law" series that ran on CBS.

**Home of Gene Barry.
[From postcard packet.
Value of packet: $3-5.]**

Lionel Barrymore (1878–1954)

Actor

Memorable Films: *The Grand Hotel* (1932); *It's a Wonderful Life* (1946).

    The role of mean businessman Henry F. Potter in the 1946 film *It's a Wonderful Life* immortalized actor Lionel Barrymore for many movie fans. Barrymore excelled when he played character parts. The Barrymore clan included his brother, actor John Barrymore, and sister, actress Ethel Barrymore. Actress Drew Barrymore continues the family tradition today.

    Beginning in the late 1920s, Barrymore resided on North Roxbury Drive in Beverly Hills.

Lionel Barrymore

Home of Lionel Barrymore. [From postcard packet. Value of packet: $3-5.]

Richard Barthelmess (1895–1963)

Actor

Memorable Films: *Way Down East* (1920); *The Dawn Patrol* (1930).

Richard Barthelmess built an impressive Hollywood resume early in his film career. His co-workers included the actresses Dorothy and Lillian Gish, and directors D.W. Griffith and Henry King. "None of the other five pictures that I did with Dick Barthelmess ever compared with *Tol'able David*," recalled King.

Richard Barthelmess

Richard Barthelmess

**Home of Richard Barthelmess. [From postcard packet.
Value of packet: $3-5.]**

12

Warner Baxter (1889–1951)

Actor

Memorable Films: *42nd Street* (1933); *The Road to Glory* (1936).

　　Warner Baxter won an Oscar for the 1929 film called *In Old Arizona*. He was named Best Actor in a Leading Role for his part as Cisco Kid in the film. Baxter used his life experiences to better his acting. "Many times in developing stage and screen characters I have reverted to the memory of some persons I have met in my travels," said Baxter. He would have mental problems to deal with in the 1940s. Baxter suffered from arthritis as well.

Home of Warner Baxter. [Value of card: $3-5.]

Madge Bellamy (1899–1990)

Actress

Memorable Films: *The Hottentot* (1922); *The Iron Horse* (1924).

Silent-star Madge Bellamy rose to Hollywood fame with her beauty in the 1920s. The actress worked with pioneering producer Thomas H. Ince. Her Hollywood career was over by the mid-1940s. By then, her personal life was in tatters, too. In 1943, Bellamy wasn't acting when she shot a man who, she claimed, was a former lover. The actress was arrested for shooting at A. Stanwood Murphy, who she said had told her just months before to "forget him." Bellamy posted bail and, shortly after, insisted that she "didn't want to hit him, but I wanted to scare him."

Madge Bellamy at home.
[Value of card: $3-5.]

Constance Bennett (1904–1965)

Actress

Memorable Films: *What Price Hollywood* (1932); *Topper* (1937).

Actress Constance Bennett made no secret of her fondness for money. "I want to be rich," she once told a reporter, "not for the luxury that wealth brings but for the independence it affords." Bennett was a thirty-thousand-dollar-a-week actress in the early 1930s. It was said to be the highest salary of any actress at the time. Actresses Joan and Barbara Bennett were her sisters.

Bennett bought a home in Los Angeles' Holmby Hills in the late 1930s.

Constance Bennett

Home of Constance Bennett. [Value of card: $8-10.]

Home of Constance Bennett. [Value of card: $8-10.]

Joan Bennett (1910–1990)

Actress

Memorable Films: *Little Women* (1933); *The Woman in the Window* (1944).

Joan Bennett had a long and successful acting career. In the late 1930s, she was earning seven thousand dollars per week. Bennett's career took off in a new direction after the 1938 film *Trade Winds*. She played a part that called for her to wear her hair black. The look was a hit, so Bennett decided to make the change more permanent. "I switched from blond to brunette," the actress recalled, "and all parts were better after that."

Joan Bennett

Home of Joan Bennett. [Value of card: $8-10.]

Jack Benny (1894–1974)

Comedian/Actor
Memorable Radio Show: *The Jack Benny Show* (1932–1955).
Memorable Television Show: "The Jack Benny Program" (1950–1965).

Comedian Jack Benny was famous for his hugely successful radio and television shows. The comedian also acted in films such as *The Big Broadcast of 1937* (1936) and *To Be or Not to Be* (1942).

Benny is closely associated with Palm Springs, where he spent many weekends during his lifetime enjoying the desert atmosphere.

Home of Jack Benny.
[Value of card: $3-5.]

Jack Benny (1894–1974) and Mary Livingstone (1905–1983)

Comedian/Actor (Benny) and Radio Personality (Livingstone)
Memorable Radio Show (Jack Benny): *The Jack Benny Show* (1932–1955).
Memorable Television Show (Jack Benny): "The Jack Benny Program" (1950–1965).
Memorable Radio Show (Mary Livingstone): *The Jack Benny Show* (1932–1955).

Jack Benny was a high school dropout, but that didn't keep him from becoming a radio and television superstar. On his radio show, his wife, Mary Livingstone, played the president of Benny's fan club.

Benny and Livingston lived in Beverly Hills on North Roxbury Drive for many years. "There were lots of people [living] only yards away, really," recalled Joan Benny, daughter of Benny and Livingstone. "At one time or another, you had Eddie Cantor, Oscar Levant, Lucille Ball, Hedy Lamarr, and Agnes Moorehead. But it wasn't that you just casually dropped in on one or another. There was a tremendous sense of personal privacy and respecting the privacy of the person across the street and next door."

Home of Jack Benny and Mary Livingstone. [Value of card: $3-5.]

Milton Berle (1908–2002)

Comedian

Memorable Films: *Always Leave Them Laughing* (1949); *It's a Mad Mad Mad Mad World* (1963).

Stage, radio, and film were all a part of the long career of entertainer Milton Berle. But it was television that would make the comedian a superstar. Berle hosted "Texaco Star Theater" for several years beginning in the late 1940s. He became known as "Uncle Miltie" to his vast television audience.

Berle lived in Beverly Hills for decades. His son, William Berle, remembered his days living in Beverly Hills. "Between the ages of two and twenty-seven, I lived in two houses," recalled William, "one on Crescent Drive and the other on Alpine Drive, a few blocks away."

Home of Milton Berle. [From postcard packet. Value of packet: $3-5.]

Home of Milton Berle. [From postcard packet. Value of packet: $3-5.]

Monte Blue (1887–1963)

Actor

Memorable Films: *Orphans of the Storm* (1921);
Kiss Me Again (1925).

    Silent-star Monte Blue was born in Indiana in 1887. Before acting, he reportedly earned a living as a coal miner and a ranch hand. Such hands-on jobs would prepare him for the stunt work he performed early in his acting career. Blue eventually became a leading man.

    In the mid-1920s, Blue moved into a home in Beverly Hills on North Camden Drive.

Monte Blue

Home of Monte Blue. [From postcard packet. Value of packet: $3-5.]

Sonny Bono (1935–1998)

Singer

Memorable Songs: "I Got You Babe" (1965); "The Beat Goes On" (1967).

Sonny Bono, part of the singing duo Sonny and Cher, not only paired with Cher on records, but in marriage as well. After splitting with Cher, Bono became an actor, a restaurateur, and a politician. A skiing accident would end Bono's life in 1998.

Bono became the mayor of the city where he owned a home, Palm Springs.

Home of Sonny Bono. [Value of card: $3-5.]

Pat Boone (1934–)

Singer

Memorable Film: *April Love* (1957).

Memorable Song: "A Wonderful Time Up There" (1958).

Singer Pat Boone became a master at generating hit records beginning in the 1950s. Prior to becoming a singing star, Boone attended Columbia University where he studied English. He recorded "Ain't That a Shame" in 1955. Boone claimed to have worried about the song's title. "I was afraid my Shakespeare professor might find out," he said in 1956.

Boone has lived in a mansion on North Beverly Drive in Beverly Hills for many years.

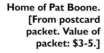

Home of Pat Boone. [From postcard packet. Value of packet: $3-5.]

Clara Bow (1907–1965)

Actress

Memorable Films: *The Plastic Age* (1925); *It* (1927).

Author Elinor Glyn created a one-word euphemism for sex appeal: "It." Actress Clara Bow had sex appeal and became the "It Girl" in the 1927 movie called *It*, which was based on a novel by Glyn. Off-screen, Bow also had a reputation as a playgirl. Screenwriter Frederica Sagor Maas worked on Bow's film, *The Plastic Age* (1925), and attended a party at her house during that time. "She giggled a lot," Maas remembered of Bow. "She was such a child—love-starved and over-sexed. Everybody took advantage of her as she climbed to stardom."

Bow purchased a North Bedford Drive home in Beverly Hills in the mid-1920s. She was at the height of her fame.

Clara Bow

Home of Clara Bow. [From postcard packet. Value of packet: $3-5.]

William Boyd (1895–1972)

Actor

Memorable Films: *The Painted Desert* (1931); *Hopalong Cassidy* (1935).

William Boyd earned fame and fortune as Hopalong Cassidy beginning in the mid-1930s. This western character served him well on film and television. Gossip columnist Hedda Hopper reported an interesting piece of William Boyd trivia in one of her syndicated columns in 1940. It read in part: "William Boyd, known to millions as 'Hopalong Cassidy,' wants a certain scene reshot in *Magic in Music*, in which his wife, Grace Bradley, plays a burlesque queen and does a striptease. Seems Bill okayed Grace's film comeback without reading the script, and now his western chivalry's boiling over…That's a nice gesture."

A Palm Desert home provided Boyd a getaway for many years beginning in the mid-1950s. An owner who had restored it put up the property for auction in 2007.

William Boyd

Home of William Boyd. [Value of card: $3-5.]

Tom Breneman (1901–1948)

Radio Host

Memorable Radio Show: *Breakfast in Hollywood* (1943–1948).

Tom Breneman was the creator and host of the radio show *Breakfast at Sardi's* (later known as *Breakfast in Hollywood*), a national hit in the 1940s. The program featured Breneman talking to Hollywood celebrities such as Bob Hope and Jimmy Durante as they ate breakfast at his namesake restaurant.

At the height of his fame, Breneman lived in the Los Angeles community of Encino.

Tom Breneman at home with his family. [Value of card: $3-5.]

The Brenemans outside their Encino home

George Burns (1896–1996) and Gracie Allen (1895–1964)

Actor (Burns) and Actress (Allen)

Memorable Films (George Allen): *The Sunshine Boys* (1975); *Oh, God!* (1977).

Memorable Film (Gracie Allen): *The Gracie Allen Murder Case* (1939).

Memorable Television Show (Gracie Allen): "The George Burns and Gracie Allen Show" (1950–1958).

Comedy actors George Burns and Gracie Allen married in 1926. They had been doing a vaudeville comedy act together since the early 1920s. In the 1950s, the couple starred in the television show, "The George Burns and Gracie Allen Show." Allen would die in 1964. Burns was famous for making light of his age toward the last decades of his life. He said he didn't believe in dying. "It's been done," quipped Burns.

Burns built a Beverly Hills home in the mid-1930s. "Having stars for parents wasn't particularly unusual in Beverly Hills," recalled Sandy Burns, daughter of Burns and Allen. "Most of our friends were children of stars."

Home of George Burns and Gracie Allen. [From postcard packet. Value of packet: $3-5.]

James Cagney (1899–1986)
Actor

Memorable Films: *The Public Enemy* (1931); *Yankee Doodle Dandy* (1942).

James Cagney could play a tough guy, a charming suitor, or a doting father with equal ease. In the mid-1930s, Cagney got a call to visit actor Charles Chaplin at his Beverly Hills mansion. Chaplin was trying to put together a movie about Napoleon and wanted Cagney to star. "I told him politely that no, I wouldn't, thinking to myself that I'd be interested in Napoleon just about as much as I'd be interested in playing Little Lord Fauntleroy," Cagney recalled.

Just as his Hollywood career was getting started in the early 1930s, Cagney moved into a North Hillcrest Drive home in Beverly Hills. The actor also bought a farm on Martha's Vineyard in the 1930s.

James Cagney

Home of James Cagney. [Value of card: $3-5.]

Home of James Cagney. [Value of card: $8-10.]

Home of James Cagney. [Value of card: $3-5.]

Eddie Cantor (1892–1964)

Actor

Memorable Films: *Whoopee* (1930); *Kid Millions* (1934).

    The stage, radio, and film were show-biz vehicles for Eddie Cantor. He appeared in *Kid Boots* with actress Clara Bow in 1926. Cantor sang "My Baby Said Yes, Yes" when he starred in *Palmy Days* (1931). He was married to his wife, Ida, for nearly five decades.

Eddie Cantor

Home of Eddie Cantor. [Value of card: $3-5.]

Helene Chadwick (1897–1940)

Actress

Memorable Films: *Wise Guys Prefer Brunettes* (1926); *Modern Mothers* (1928).

Before she turned to acting, Helene Chadwick was a model who made the cover of *Harrison Fisher* magazine several times. In 1916, Chadwick began to act in silent films. Chadwick would marry and divorce the director William Wellman before he directed the silent-film classic, *Wings* (1927).

Chadwick once lived in a courtyard apartment complex.

830:—Residence of Helen Chadwick, Hollywood, Calif.

Home of Helene Chadwick. [Value of card: $3-5.]

Lon Chaney (1883–1930)

Actor

Memorable Films: *The Phantom of the Opera* (1925); *Laugh Clown, Laugh* (1928).

Lon Chaney, an actor who also pioneered many movie make-up techniques, was known as "The Man of a Thousand Faces." His face appeared in many classic silent pictures. In the 1923 film *The Hunchback of Notre Dame* Chaney played the part of Quasimodo. He was Erik, The Phantom in *The Phantom of the Opera* (1925). Film fans would find it hard to imagine anybody but Chaney in these roles. The actor died wealthy at the age of forty-seven.

A modest home on North Linden Drive in Beverly Hills was where Chaney lived during his movie star days. He moved out of the home before his death in 1930.

830   RESIDENCE OF LON CHANEY, BEVERLY HILLS, CALIFORNIA

5030-29

Home of Lon Chaney. [Value of card: $3-5.]

Charles Chaplin (1889–1977)

Actor

Memorable Films: *The Gold Rush* (1925); *City Lights* (1931).

Charles Chaplin is still considered by many to be Hollywood's consummate comic genius. Shortly after he began acting in films in 1914, Chaplin began to handle every aspect of nearly every movie he was involved in. He ultimately produced and directed most of his films. Chaplin's second wife, Lita Grey, was found earning a living at a department store decades after divorcing the actor. The store was located in Beverly Hills where Grey had once lived in luxury with Chaplin.

Charles Chaplin

"One afternoon as I was driving past Charlie's house, I saw his two boys, Sydney and Charles, Jr., out front with a lemonade stand. They were doing a thriving business serving workmen from the adjoining lot, where another new house was going up. It wasn't a hot day, and I wondered why the long line. I soon found out. I parked the car and joined the line. When my turn came, Charles, Jr. filled a glass for me from the pitcher, saying, 'Five cents, please.' It was pure Scotch."

—Actress Colleen Moore

Home of Charles Chaplin. [From postcard packet. Value of packet: $3-5.]

Sydney Chaplin (1885–1965)

Actor

Memorable Films: *Shoulder Arms* (1914); *The Pilgrim* (1923).

Actor and movie-businessman Sydney Chaplin was the half brother of actor Charles Chaplin. He was tapped by his famous brother, who was younger, to become his manager. The Chaplins grew up poor in England and would do whatever it took to help their struggling mother keep the household afloat. "Sydney sold newspapers between school hours, and though his contribution was less than a drop in the bucket, it did give a modicum of aid," recalled his famous younger brother.

Chaplin's corner-lot mansion was located close to his brother's company building, the Chaplin Studio on La Brea Avenue in Hollywood.

**Sydney Chaplin at home.
[From postcard packet.
Value of packet: $3-5.]**

Cher (1946–)

Singer

Memorable Songs: "You Better Sit Down Kids" (1967); "Take Me Home" (1979).

Cher was part of the singing pair Sonny and Cher. The two were married before their 1965 hit record "I Got You Babe" was released. Sonny and Cher broke-up as an act and a married couple in the 1970s.

**Home of Cher.
[From postcard
packet. Value of
packet: $3-5.]**

30

Lew Cody (1884–1934)

Actor

Memorable Films: *The Mating* (1915); *Rupert of Hentzau* (1923).

You may not find an entry for silent-star Lew Cody in recently published movie-star reference books. He is one of the industry's forgotten stars, despite appearing in nearly one hundred films and marrying one of Hollywood's historic figures, actress Mabel Normand. Comedic silent-film star Buster Keaton once did stunt work for Cody in *The Baby Cyclone* (1928). "Well, Cody can't fall off a chair without putting himself in [the] hospital," Keaton later joked.

Lew Cody

Home of Lew Cody. [Value of card: $3-5.]

Claudette Colbert (1903–1996)

Actress

Memorable Films: *It Happened One Night* (1934); *Palm Beach Story* (1942).

Paris-born Claudette Colbert was directed by legendary director Frank Capra in her first film, *For the Love of Mike* (1927). She did not like her initial forays into films. Despite her first impressions, Colbert did not give up on Hollywood. She would become a star. Colbert once summed up the roles she played by saying, "There's nothing less interesting than a goody-goody, and I played a lot of them." She added, "The best thing to play is a bitch with a heart of gold."

In the 1930s, Colbert moved into her mansion in the Holmby Hills area of Los Angeles.

Claudette Colbert

Home of Claudette Colbert. [Value of card: $3-5.]

Chuck Connors (1921–1992)

Actor

Memorable Television Show: "The Rifleman" (1958–1963).

Chuck Connors handled baseballs and basketballs for money as a professional athlete. The actor handled a rifle when he starred in a television series. Beginning in 1958, Connors played Lucas McCain on television's "The Rifleman" series. "Westerns aren't going to die," Connors said just weeks before the series debuted. "Some of them will go off the air, but the good ones will last. And, we've got a good one."

Connors had a Palm Springs home from the early 1960s to the early 1970s.

Chuck Connors

Home of Chuck
Connors. [Value of
card: $3-5.]

Jackie Coogan (1914–1984)

Actor

Memorable Films: *The Kid* (1921); *The Joker Is Wild* (1947).

Jackie Coogan was on film before Charles Chaplin took notice of him on a stage. But Chaplin made Coogan an instant child star by casting him in his movie, *The Kid* (1921). Coogan was no kid when it came to being inventive on the set. When he had trouble crying for a scene in *Oliver Twist* (1922), he asked the director if it would "be all right if I imagine my dog is dead." Coogan is also famous for being forced to file suit in the 1930s against his own parents to recover his film earnings they held. He ended up gaining only a fraction of the earnings.

Coogan lived in a palace-like home as a child actor.

Jackie Coogan and
his home. [Value of
card: $7-9.]

Gary Cooper (1901–1961)

Actor

Memorable Films: *The Pride of the Yankees* (1942); *High Noon* (1952).

It is hard to think of Gary Cooper as a silent-film actor, but that is where he began his screen acting career. Cooper made a strong impression on audiences and Hollywood executives with his small part in the 1927 film, *Wings*. His career took off with talking pictures. Cooper died a wealthy man, which probably didn't surprise those who knew that he could be tightfisted with cash. After he became wealthy, Cooper once asked screenwriter Jesse Lasky, Jr. to have a soft drink with him after they'd finished some dialog adjustment for a film. After depositing two nickels into a drink machine, Cooper pulled out a couple of cokes. He then handed one to Lasky, Jr. saying, "Yours is five cents, Jess."

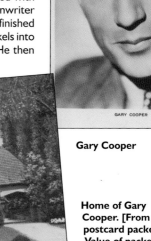

Gary Cooper

Home of Gary Cooper. [From postcard packet. Value of packet: $3-5.]

Lou Costello (1906–1959)

Actor

Memorable Films: *Buck Privates* (1941); *Africa Screams* (1949).

A comedy pairing in the 1930s would make Lou Costello a household name by the 1940s. He teamed with comic straight-man Bud Abbott to form the duo, Abbott and Costello. In the 1940s, the team made a string of popular movies featuring antics such as their famous routine, "Who's on First?" In 1958, the comedy star was fined and placed on summary probation by a judge for a leash-law violation. After the court proceedings ended, he was asked by the judge, "Tell me, who's on second?" Costello replied, "The dog."

Costello owned a home in Sherman Oaks, a community in the San Fernando Valley area of Los Angeles.

Home of Lou Costello. [From postcard packet. Value of packet: $3-5.]

Joan Crawford (1905–1977)

Actress

Memorable Films: *Strange Cargo* (1940); *Mildred Pierce* (1945).

Actress Joan Crawford started her film career in the mild-1920s with bit parts but quickly became a star. Screenwriter Frederica Sagor Maas got to know Crawford when the two worked at MGM. Crawford would eat lunch with Maas and others in the commissary at MGM. "But she was a loner and did not make friends easily," Maas said of Crawford. "She was distrustful of everyone, including herself."

Crawford's Brentwood house on North Bristol Avenue is known as the "Mommie Dearest Home." Daughter Christina Crawford wrote a well-known book called *Mommie Dearest: A True Story* about her less than happy childhood.

Joan Crawford

Home of Joan Crawford, Brentwood, California

Home of Joan Crawford. [From postcard packet. Value of packet: $3-5.]

Bing Crosby (1903–1977)

Singer/Actor

Memorable Film: *The Road to Utopia* (1946).

Memorable Song: "White Christmas" (1942).

Bing Crosby

As an actor, Bing Crosby was one of Paramount Pictures' big stars in the 1930s. His easygoing and approachable public image did not match his true personality. Fans would often find Crosby cold and rude when they approached him. He also was drinking heavily as his film career was taking off at Paramount.

Crosby had a home on Forman Avenue in the Toluca Lake area of Los Angeles, where he lived with his wife, actress Dixie Lee, in the 1930s. But he moved to a North Hollywood, Colonial-revival style mansion in the mid-1930s. "The children kept coming, so we had to build a bigger one," explained Crosby. Also in the 1930s, Crosby bought a home on a huge piece of property in Rancho Santa Fe, California.

Home of Bing Crosby. [Value of card: $8-10.]

Home of Bing Crosby. [Value of card: $8-10.]

James Cruze (1884–1942) and Betty Compson (1897–1974).

Director (Cruze) and Actress (Compson)

Memorable Films (James Cruze, as director): *The Covered Wagon* (1923); *I Cover the Waterfront* (1933).

Memorable Films (Betty Compson): *Paths to Paradise* (1925); *The Docks of New York* (1928).

Actor, producer, and director were all job titles held by James Cruze. The bulk of his Hollywood work was confined to the silent-film era. He would marry silent-star Betty Compson, a fellow Utah native, in the mid-1920s. The couple would divorce in 1930.

Betty Compson

Home of James Cruze and Betty Compson. [Value of card: $3-5.]

Tony Curtis (1925–)

Actor

Memorable Films: *The Sweet Smell of Success* (1957); *Some Like It Hot* (1959).

Born in New York, Tony Curtis proved himself to be a versatile actor. He was equally convincing in the biographical film, *Houdini* (1953), as he was in the comedy, *Some Like It Hot* (1959). In the early 1950s, actress Janet Leigh became Curtis's first wife.

Curtis once lived in a home that is located on a cul-de-sac in Beverly Hills.

Home of Tony Curtis. [From postcard packet. Value of packet: $3-5.]

Bebe Daniels (1901–1971)

Actress

Memorable Films: *Monsieur Beaucaire* (1924); *Music Is Magic* (1935).

Actress Bebe Daniels was just a child when she started appearing in films. Daniels would make news as a teenage actress in March 1921 when she became the first woman in Orange County, California, to be convicted of speeding in a car. She was sentenced to ten days in jail for the infraction. "I'll never speed again as long as I live," announced Daniels upon her release from jail.

Bebe Daniels

Home of Bebe Daniels. [Value of card: $3-5.]

Marion Davies (1897–1961)

Actress

Memorable Films: *The Patsy* (1928); *Show People* (1928).

Blond-haired Marion Davies began film acting in the silent era. Those who study her career find that all roads lead to William Randolph Hearst. She would do most of her acting for Hearst's film company. He would hold her back from possibly becoming a comedy superstar by placing her in dramatic films that required her to wear over-the-top costume pieces. Still, late in life Davies wrote that she was fond of Hearst, whom she called W.R. "I was always on W.R.'s side, so there was nothing to argue about," said Davies. "And W.R. was always on my side. That's why I liked him so much."

Davies was a longtime resident of Beverly Hills. The first home she bought in the city was on Lexington Road.

Marion Davies

Home of Marion Davies. [From postcard packet. Value of packet: $3-5.]

Bette Davis (1908–1989)

Actress

Memorable Films: *Now Voyager* (1942); *All About Eve* (1950).

Bette Davis starred in a long list of classic films, including *Jezebel* (1938), *The Little Foxes* (1941), and *Whatever Happened to Baby Jane?* (1962). Audiences may have enjoyed her work in films, but Davis didn't. "I never could *bear* myself on the screen," said Davis.

Davis moved to a Tudor-style home in North Hollywood in the late 1930s.

Bette Davis

Home of Bette Davis. [Value of card: $3-5.]

Doris Day (1924–)

Singer/Actress

Memorable Film: *Please Don't Eat the Daisies* (1960).

Memorable Song: "Sentimental Journey" (1945).

Doris Day was already a successful singer when Hollywood would come calling in the late 1940s. When considering Day's screen image, clean-cut, perky, and wholesome are words that come to mind. In the mid-1970s, actor Rock Hudson, a good friend of Day's, speculated on the reason for her longtime squeaky-clean image. "She had a soda fountain in her home instead of a bar," he said.

Home of Doris Day. [From postcard packet. Value of packet: $3-5.]

In the early 1960s, Day and her husband, Marty Melcher, moved into a home in Beverly Hills that they had purchased. Day would continue to live in the home for years after the couple divorced in the late 1960s.

Home of Doris Day. [Value of card: $3-5.]

Dolores Del Rio (1905–1983)

Actress

Memorable Films: *What Price Glory* (1926); *Flying Down to Rio* (1933).

Dolores Del Rio

Born in Mexico, actress Dolores Del Rio came to America in 1925. Del Rio may have been the most exotic female beauty to ever grace the screen. She quickly found America to her liking. "I am in love with Los Angeles," declared Del Rio in 1926. "America has been most kind to me and I appreciate it. I feel I can show my feelings in no better way than to apply for permanent residence in this glorious land," said the actress.

An Outpost Drive home in the Outpost Estates area of Los Angeles was built by Del Rio in the late 1920s. The actress had the mansion designed to duplicate a Mexico City villa she had loved when she was a child.

Dolores Del Rio at home. [Value of card: $3-5.]

Dolores Del Rio at home. [Value of card: $3-5.]

William Desmond (1878–1949)

Actor

Memorable Films: *The Prodigal Liar* (1919); *Perils of the Yukon* (1922).

Born in Dublin, Ireland, William Desmond became a cowboy star in the silent-film era. Desmond acted on stage at the Burbank Theatre in Los Angeles before entering films.

Home of William Desmond. [From postcard packet. Value of packet: $3-5.]

Andy Devine (1905–1977)

Actor

Memorable Film: *Stagecoach* (1939).

Memorable Television Show: "Adventures of Wild Bill Hickok" (1951–1958).

Andy Devine was a heavyset character actor with a distinctive voice. Among his many western roles was that of Deputy Marshal P. Jingles on television's "Adventures of Wild Bill Hickok," which ran in the 1950s.

Beginning in the 1930s, Devine served as an honorary mayor of Van Nuys, a Los Angeles community where he had a home. Devine enjoyed the job. "Golly if ma and pa could only see me now," said the gravel-voiced actor after being named to his third term.

Home of Andy Devine. [Value of card: $8-10.]

Marlene Dietrich (1901–1992)

Actress

Memorable Films: *The Blue Angel* (1932); *Witness for the Prosecution* (1957).

Marlene Dietrich began her acting career in the 1920s in her native Germany. As a Hollywood star, Dietrich attracted attention in public, even when other stars were present. Actress Betsy Blair attended the 1955 Cannes Film Festival. Blair recalled "One day on the Croisette I saw a storm of photographers running and shouting—they'd obviously spotted some great star. It was Marlene Dietrich." Dietrich had become a mysterious figure of sorts toward the end of her life. She was rarely seen in public.

Dietrich began calling North Roxbury Drive in Beverly Hills home in the early 1930s.

Marlene Dietrich

Home of Marlene Dietrich. [Value of card: $8-10.]

Phyllis Diller (1917–)

Comedian

Memorable Films: *Boy, Did I Get a Wrong Number?* (1966); *A Bug's Life* (1998).

Phyllis Diller has performed comedy as a stand-up act, in movies, and on television. She didn't perform her first comic stage routine until she was in her late 30s

The Los Angeles community of Brentwood has been Diller's longtime home.

"You know the best way to double your money? Fold it and put it in your pocket."

—Phyllis Diller

**Home of Phyllis Diller.
[From postcard packet.
Value of packet: $3-5.]**

Richard Dix (1893–1949)

Actor

Memorable Films: *The Ten Commandments* (1923); *Cimarron* (1931).

Richard Dix was a silent star in the 1920s, but was relegated to "B" films before his Hollywood career was over in the 1940s. The six-foot-tall Dix studied medicine before turning to acting.

Richard Dix

**Home of Richard Dix.
[Value of card: $3-5.]**

Kirk Douglas (1916–)

Actor

Memorable Films: *Lust for Life* (1956); *Strangers When We Meet* (1960).

Kirk Douglas's cleft chin became a physical trademark that gave him a distinctive look that fans loved. Off-screen, some of his real-life qualities matched his tough-guy roles. Douglas wrestled in college and joined the U.S. Navy in the early 1940s.

In the late 1950s, Douglas bought a home in Beverly Hills and would stay there for many years.

Kirk Douglas

Home of Kirk Douglas.
[Value of card: $3-5.]

Home of Kirk Douglas.
[From postcard packet.
Value of packet: $3-5.]

Billie Dove (1903–1997)

Actress

Memorable Films: *Wanderer of the Wasteland* (1924); *The Black Pirate* (1926).

When she was still a teenager, Billie Dove appeared on stage in the Ziegfeld Follies. She opted for Hollywood in the early 1920s and became a screen star. Dove's film career lasted about a decade.

Billie Dove

Home of Billie Dove. [Value of card: $3-5.]

Faye Dunaway (1941–)

Actress

Memorable Films: *Bonnie and Clyde* (1967); *Three Days of the Condor* (1975).

Faye Dunaway won an Oscar for Best Actress in a Leading Role for her work in *Network* (1976). In the 1981 film, *Mommie Dearest*, Dunaway played the role of actress Joan Crawford. "She's the most frightening of all the ladies I've played, because of her intensity," said Dunaway.

Home of Faye Dunaway. [From postcard packet. Value of packet: $3-5.]

Irene Dunne (1898–1990)

Actress

Memorable Films: *The Awful Truth* (1936); *My Favorite Wife* (1940).

Irene Dunne proved to be a versatile actress who was equally at home in comedies, dramas, and musicals. Dunne earned an Academy Award nomination for playing opposite Richard Dix in the 1931 film, *Cimarron*. Actor Douglas Fairbanks, Jr., who worked with Dunne, called her "one of the most professional women I've ever known."

Irene Dunne

**Home of Irene Dunne.
[Value of card: $3-5.]**

Jimmy Durante (1893–1980)

Actor/Entertainer

Memorable Films: *You're in the Army Now* (1941); *It's a Mad Mad Mad Mad World* (1963).

Jimmy Durante was not just a man with a famous nose. He could entertain in a variety of settings, including the stage, radio, film, and television. Friends and fans called him "The Schnozzola," making good-natured fun of his huge nose. Durante became famous for his 1934 hit song, "Inka Dinka Doo."

**Home of Jimmy
Durante. [Value
of card: $3-5.]**

Deanna Durbin (1921–)

Actress

Memorable Films: *Mad About Music* (1938); *It Started With Eve* (1941).

Born in Canada, Deanna Durbin had originally planned to pursue a career as an opera singer. But Universal Pictures put her face and voice onto film in 1930s musicals. The actress tired of Hollywood and vanished from the screen in the late 1940s.

Deanna Durbin

Home of Deanna Durbin. [Value of card: $14-16.]

Douglas Fairbanks (1883–1939) and Mary Pickford (1892–1979)

Actor (Fairbanks) and Actress (Pickford)

Memorable Films (Douglas Fairbanks): *Robin Hood* (1922); *The Thief of Bagdad* (1924).

Memorable Films (Mary Pickford): *Rebecca of Sunnybrook Farm* (1917); *Sparrows* (1926).

There was plenty of action and adventure in films that featured Douglas Fairbanks. He played roles such as Robin Hood, Zorro, and The Thief of Bagdad that demonstrated his athletic talents. Fairbanks married actress Mary Pickford in 1920 and they became one of Hollywood's most celebrated couplings. Pickford, a.k.a. "America's Sweetheart," was raised in poverty. When she died in 1979, she was worth millions. Pickford was known for her business savvy—a trait that, according to some Hollywood observers, threatened her innocent screen image. "I'm not the money-lover that I sound," Pickford once declared in her own defense. Even so, actor Charles Chaplin irked Pickford when he tagged her "Bank of America's Sweetheart."

Douglas Fairbanks and Mary Pickford

On their wedding night in 1920, Fairbanks gave Pickford a mansion in Beverly Hills. "This house," proclaimed Fairbanks, "is yours, Mary. It's my wedding present to you." The home was called Pickfair.

"I didn't like Pickfair, the home Mary Pickford and Douglas Fairbanks had built. I might like it now, but it was no garden of earthly delights for a kid. It was cold, deathly quiet, uncomfortable both physically and spiritually to me. I had been in the White House and found that much more homey than Pickfair. I remember thinking, when I was shown into the living room, that I was the first human being who had ever set foot in the place."

—Actor Jackie Cooper, who visited the mansion in the mid-1930s when he was a child star.

Home of Douglas Fairbanks and Mary Pickford. [Value of card: $8-10.]

Mary and Douglas Fairbanks Residence, Los Angeles, California

Home of Douglas Fairbanks and Mary Pickford. [Value of card: $3-5.]

Douglas Fairbanks, Jr. (1909–2000)

Actor

Memorable Films: *Little Caesar* (1930); *Gunga Din* (1939).

Douglas Fairbanks Jr. had a famous father, step-mother, and first wife. The dad and step mom were silent-screen superstars Douglas Fairbanks and Mary Pickford, respectively. And, his famous first wife was actress Joan Crawford, whom he married in 1929. The couple divorced in early 1933.

When his Hollywood career was starting to pick-up steam, Fairbanks, Jr. was living in Beverly Hills.

Douglas Fairbanks, Jr.

HOME OF THE DOUGLAS FAIRBANKS, JR. (JOAN CRAWFORD) BEVERLY HILLS, CALIF.   A-102

Home of Douglas Fairbanks, Jr. (Card erroneously places Joan Crawford as a resident.) [Value of card: $3-5.]

Peter Falk (1927–)

Actor
Memorable Film: *Murder, Inc.* (1960).
Memorable Television Show: "Columbo" (1971–1977).

Actor Peter Falk was born in New York City, but he would roam Los Angeles as Lieutenant Columbo for television's "Columbo." Fans would be hard pressed to find anybody else who could have played the role as convincingly as Falk did.

Falk has lived for many years in Beverly Hills.

Home of Peter Falk. [From postcard packet. Value of packet: $3-5.]

Dustin Farnum (1874–1929)

Actor

Memorable Films: *The Squaw Man* (1914); *The Virginian* (1914).

Dustin Farnum was a stage and silent-film actor. Director Jay Hunt remembered when a young Farnum was a stage manager for a Broadway theater.

"One day while we were looking around for someone to fill small, unimportant parts in the stock company, a likeable looking lad came in and we employed him," recalled Hunt, adding, "Dustin Farnum even then showed promise." In 1924, Farnum asked for a divorce from his second wife, Mary. He claimed Mary had deserted him by refusing to move with him from New York to Los Angeles, he told the court. On the witness stand, Farnum was asked if he tried hard to get Mary to come to California with him. "Yes," said Farnum, "as far as my dignity would permit." The divorce was granted.

834:—Home of Dustin Farnum, near Los Angeles, Calif.

17608

Home of Dustin Farnum. [Value of card: $3-5.]

William Farnum (1876–1953)

Actor

Memorable Films: *A Tale of Two Cities* (1917); *If I Were King* (1920).

When it came to acting on film, William Farnum was workhorse. His career started during the earliest years of the silent-film era and ended in the 1950s. It has been said that the actor was the first film star to earn ten thousand dollars a week. Farnum was the brother of actor Dustin Farnum and director Marshall Farnum. During his 1953 funeral, actor Pat O'Brien gave a eulogy. "I see a great homecoming for Bill through those pearly gates," spoke O'Brien. "Greeting him will be his brother Dusty and all his old friends—Barrymore, Booth, Drew, Eddie Foy, Modjeska, Sam Hardy, Cohan, Harris."

Home of William Farnum. [Value of card: $3-5.]

Charles Farrell (1901–1990)

Actor

Memorable Films: *Street Angel* (1928); *The Man Who Came Back* (1931).

Instrumental in making actor Charles Farrell a star was his pairing up with Janet Gaynor on the silver screen beginning in the late 1920s. The two would star opposite each other in many films, starting with the romantic film *Seventh Heaven* (1927). By the early 1940s, Farrell was out of the picture business. He made an acting comeback by co-starring in television's "My Little Margie" in the 1950s.

Charles Farrell

Home of Charles Farrell. [Value of card: $3-5.]

Eddie Fisher (1928–)
Singer
Memorable Songs: "Lady of Spain" (1952); "I Need You Now" (1954).

In the 1950s, Eddie Fisher had a string of hit records. During his lifetime, he has collected a string of famous wives, including actresses Debbie Reynolds, Elizabeth Taylor, and Connie Stevens. They are all now Fisher's ex-wives.

Home of Eddie Fisher. [Value of card: $3-5.]

Eddie Fisher (1928–) and Debbie Reynolds (1932–)

Singer (Fisher) and Actress (Reynolds)
Memorable Songs (Eddie Fisher): "Any Time" (1952); "Oh! My Pa-Pa" (1953).
Memorable Films (Debbie Reynolds): *Singin' in the Rain* (1952); *The Unsinkable Molly Brown* (1964).

Pennsylvania-born Eddie Fisher was raised in humble surroundings, but became a record-chart topper in the 1950s. Musicals of the 1950s made actress Debbie Reynolds a film star. Fisher married Reynolds in 1955. Reynolds described their 1954 engagement party given by Ida and Eddie Cantor at the Beverly Hills Hotel. "Eddie Cantor, being like an adopted father to Eddie, invited all his old show-business friends including Jack Benny, Jack Warner, and Groucho Marx. There were MGM stars, friends from the industry, the major newspaper columnists, all of Eddie's pals from South Philadelphia, and all of my friends, including school chums Jeanette Johnson and Camille Williams. There were forty-five photographers present and every one of them wanted a picture of me and Eddie kissing. The following week, *Life* magazine did a four-page layout of the party," Reynolds recalled.

Home of Eddie Fisher and Debbie Reynolds. [Value of card: $3-5.]

Alec Francis (1867–1934)

Actor
Memorable Films: *Smilin' Through* (1922); *Arrowsmith* (1931).

Actor Alec Francis appeared in two-hundred-plus films, but his name has faded from public memory. The actor once lost his own sense of himself during the early 1930s when he suffered a bout of amnesia. Police found Francis walking on a highway in Ventura, about sixty miles from his home. After returning from a Ventura hospital where he received care, Francis was ready to return to movie making. "I feel fit and am certain that I will be back on the lot within a few days," stated Francis.

Home of Alec Francis. [Value of card: $3-5.]

Home was once North Cahuenga Avenue in Hollywood for Francis.

Pauline Frederick (1883–1938)

Actress

Memorable Films: *Smouldering Fires* (1924); *Wayward* (1932).

Pauline Frederick gained fame on stage and screen. Actress Laura La Plante worked with Frederick. "She was to me a great actress," said La Plante, "I felt like an amateur with her." Frederick's silent-star days peaked in the early 1920s. Fredrick's real-life romances did not produce a pretty picture. Of her five marriages, four ended in divorce. Frederick died from an asthmatic condition in 1938. Her death made the front page of the *Los Angeles Times*.

Frederick owned a mansion on Sunset Boulevard in Beverly Hills. In 1927, actress Norma Shearer and her new husband, MGM executive Irving Thalberg, leased the home from Frederick.

Pauline Frederick

Miss Fredericks holds her audience spellbound with her rare artistry. She is famously noted for her characterizations of fascinating and alluring women, as well as for her realistic portrayals of sweet, innocent girlhood. Her many notable screen successes have won her the unqualified approval of admiring photoplay enthusiasts.

Cahill-Igoe Company, Chicago, Publishers

Pauline Frederick

Home of Pauline Frederick, Beverly Hills, California.

Home of Pauline Frederick. [Value of card: $3-5.]

Clark Gable (1901–1960)

Actor

Memorable Films: *It Happened One Night* (1934); *Gone With the Wind* (1939).

After collecting eleven thousand dollars for work in a William Boyd film, actor Clark Gable was heard to say, "No actor's worth that!" Early in his film career, Gable didn't expect Hollywood to be good to him for long. "This can't last," is how Gable put it to Ralph Bellamy while they were shooting *The Secret Six* (1931). It did last and Gable became one of the most famous stars in the world.

"Clark Gable always has champagne with everything, lots of it, the best, Perrier-Jouët or Bollinger in double bottles and ice-cold."

—Restaurateur Michael Romanoff who founded Romanoffs restaurant in Beverly Hills.

Birthplace of Clark Gable. [Value of card: $3-5.]

Home of Clark Gable. [Value of card: $3-5.]

Home of Clark Gable. [From postcard packet. Value of packet: $3-5.]

Richard "Skeets" Gallagher (1891–1955)

Actor

Memorable Films: *Up Pops the Devil* (1931); *Too Much Harmony* (1933).

Comic actor Richard "Skeets" Gallagher started his career in vaudeville. He next took his talents to the silver screen, playing leading roles and many supporting characters. Gallagher's nickname, "Skeets," was short for "Mosquito," a named he earned in childhood from his habit of darting around speedily.

HOME OF "SKEETS" GALLAGHER, BEVERLY HILLS, CALIFORNIA   BH9

BEAUTIFUL HOMES OF SOUTHERN CALIFORNIA

Home of Richard "Skeets" Gallagher. [Value of card: $3-5.]

Judy Garland (1922–1969)

Singer/Actress

Memorable Films: *The Wizard of Oz* (1939); *Meet Me in St. Louis* (1944).

Almost anybody over a certain age instantly recalls actress Judy Garland when they hear the song "Somewhere Over the Rainbow." She sang it as the character Dorothy in *The Wizard of Oz* (1939), and it became the movie's signature song. Director/writer Joseph Mankiewicz described Garland as "the most remarkably bright, gay, happy, helpless, and engaging girl." In 1984, Garland memorabilia was still in demand, at least by thieves. Three men were arrested after they attempted to steal Garland memorabilia at the home of Sidney Luft, Garland's third husband.

Judy Garland

Home of Judy Garland. [Value of card: $3-5.]

Janet Gaynor (1906–1984)

Actress

Memorable Films: *Sunrise* (1927); *A Star Is Born* (1937).

    Both silent and talking pictures were good to actress Janet Gaynor. At the first Academy Awards ceremony, held in 1929, Gaynor took home the award for Best Actress in a Leading Role. It was for a collection of films, as was often the case for awards that were presented during the early history of the Oscars. Actor Charles Farrell and Gaynor were a successful Hollywood movie team in many romantic films.

Janet Gaynor

Janet Gaynor

Home of Janet Gaynor. [Value of card: $3-5.]

Janet Gaynor at home. [Value of card: $3-5.]

Mitzi Gaynor (1931–)

Actress

Memorable Films: *The Joker Is Wild* (1957); *South Pacific* (1958).

Mitzi Gaynor sang and danced her way to stardom in the 1950s. The 1958 film, *South Pacific*, was a career highlight for Gaynor. She later worked with many big-name stars such as Marilyn Monroe and Gene Kelly.

Gaynor and husband, producer and agent Jack Bean, moved into a house on North Arden Drive in Beverly Hills in 1960.

Home of Mitzi Gaynor. [From postcard packet. Value of packet: $3-5.]

Hoot Gibson (1892–1962)

Actor
Memorable Films: *Smilin' Kid* (1920); *Cavalcade of the West* (1936).

Cowboy actor Hoot Gibson started drawing huge audiences in the silent-film era. He could ride a horse with expertise, both on and off screen. Early in his career, Gibson worked with legendary directors D.W. Griffith and Francis Boggs. Despite his many years on the screen, Gibson had financial difficulties toward the end of his life.

In the mid-1920s, Gibson moved into a home on North Bedford Drive in Beverly Hills.

Hoot Gibson

Home of Hoot Gibson.
[From postcard packet.
Value of packet: $3-5.]

Freeman Gosden (1899–1982)

Radio Actor
Memorable Film: *The Big Broadcast of 1936* (1935).
Memorable Radio Show: *Amos 'n' Andy* (1928–1955).

Freeman Gosden played the character of Amos Jones on the famous radio program, *Amos 'n' Andy*. The character of Andrew "Andy" Brown was played by Charles Correll. The program aired for many years starting in the late 1920s.

Home of Freeman
Gosden. [Value of
card: $8-10.]

Cary Grant (1904–1986)

Actor

Memorable Films: *The Philadelphia Story* (1940); *North by Northwest* (1959).

A charming star of numerous classic pictures, actor Cary Grant could be difficult to be around in person. Grant closely guarded both his image and his money. He was a notorious tightwad. Being financially conservative ultimately paid off for one of Hollywood's most famous leading men. Grant would die worth tens of millions of dollars.

Grant loved to ride horses in Palm Springs, where he bought a home in the 1950s.

"All any producer had to do was to tell me his proposed film had Cary Grant as the male star, and I'd be there with bells on!"

—Actress Ginger Rogers

Home of Cary Grant. [Value of card: $3-5.]

Home of Cary Grant. [Value of card: $3-5.]

Ann Harding (1901–1981)
Actress
Memorable Films: *Her Private Affair* (1929); *The Man in the Grey Flannel Suit* (1956).

Texas-born actress Ann Harding was a leading lady on the Broadway stage and on the silver screen. Harding appeared frequently on television from the early 1950s to the mid-1960s.

Home of Ann Harding. [Value of card: $3-5.]

Oliver Hardy (1892–1957)

Actor

Memorable Films: *Big Business* (1929); *Sons of the Desert* (1933).

Oliver Hardy was half—the physically bigger half—of the comedy-film duo, Laurel and Hardy. He and actor Stan Laurel made over twenty feature films as a team. Their first feature, made in 1931, was *Pardon Us*. When Hardy died in 1957, Laurel took it hard. "What's there to say?" Laurel was quoted as saying. "He was like a brother. That's the end of the history of Laurel and Hardy."

Oliver Hardy

Home of Oliver Hardy.
[Value of card: $8-10.]

Kenneth Harlan (1895–1967) and Marie Prevost (1898–1937)

Actor (Harlan) and Actress (Prevost)

Memorable Films (Kenneth Harlan): *Lessons in Love* (1921); *The Toll of the Sea* (1922).

Memorable Films (Marie Prevost): *Getting Gertie's Garter* (1927); *The Racket* (1928).

The Hollywood career of Marie Prevost would start and finish with a struggle to find decent parts. The Canadian-born Prevost became a busy actress in the 1920s after years of trying to get noticed. She and actor Kenneth Harlan were briefly married in the mid-1920s. Harlan was a leading man during the silent-screen era, but his film days ended by the 1940s. Prevost's life didn't have a Hollywood-happy ending. The one-time Mack Sennett bathing beauty was found dead in a Hollywood apartment that was littered with empty whiskey bottles. Prevost was thirty-eight years old.

Home of Kenneth Harlan and Marie Prevost. [Value of card: $3-5.]

Jean Harlow (1911–1937)

Actress

Memorable Films: *Red Dust* (1932); *Dinner at Eight* (1933).

Actress Jean Harlow became an acting sensation in the 1930s. But the star was well known for many things besides acting. Harlow, a platinum blonde, married screenwriter Paul Bern, who committed suicide shortly afterward. Harlow herself died young, at age twenty-six. Despite her brief career, Harlow's name and image are still recognized throughout the world.

Jean Harlow

Home of Jean Harlow.
[Value of card: $3-5.]

Home of Jean Harlow. [From postcard packet. Value of packet: $3-5.]

William S. Hart (1865–1946)

Actor

Memorable Films: *Branding Broadway* (1918); *Tumbleweeds* (1928).

Popular cowboy actor William S. Hart appeared in western plays before turning to the silent screen. He was in his mid-forties when he first appeared in films. Hart directed many of his own films. Hart's movie career was over by 1925. He was financially well off when he died in 1946.

William S. Hart

Home of William S. Hart. [From postcard packet. Value of packet: $3-5.]

Home of William S. Hart. [Value of card: $3-5.]

Home of William S. Hart. [Value of card: $3-5.]

Goldie Hawn (1945–)

Actress

Memorable Films: *Butterflies are Free* (1972); *Private Benjamin* (1980).

Goldie Hawn became famous in the late 1960s as a joke-telling blonde in a skimpy bikini on television's "Laugh In" comedy show. She parlayed her television success into a film career. Hawn won an Academy Award for Best Supporting Actress for her part in the 1969 film *Cactus Flower*.

**Home of Goldie Hawn.
[From postcard packet.
Value of packet: $3-5.]**

Sessue Hayakawa (1889–1973)

Actor

Memorable Films: *The Cheat* (1915); *The Bridge on the River Kwai* (1957).

Before coming to America as a teenager, actor Sessue Hayakawa did some stage work in Japan, where he was born. His talents were eventually noticed by Hollywood. Hayakawa would become the first major Asian Hollywood star. He was paid well as an actor and starred in over eighty films. Actress Tsuru Aoki was his wife.

The Sessue Hayakawa Home, Los Angeles, California.

Sessue Hayakawa

Home of Sessue Hayakawa. [Value of card: $4-6.]

Sessue Hayakawa

69

Helen Hayes (1900–1993)

Actress

Memorable Films: *Arrowsmith* (1931); *Fare-well to Arms* (1932).

Baby Boomers know actress Helen Hayes from her many television roles, but her impressive stage and film career are all but forgotten. Hayes has been called "The First Lady of the American Theater," a title she has shared with actress Ethel Barrymore.

Hayes's Nyack, New York, mansion was called Pretty Penny. She and her husband, screenwriter and playwright Charles MacArthur, bought it in the 1930s. "Charles Lederer, Marion Davies' nephew, called our house 'Pretty Penny,' because that's what he supposed it had cost," said Hayes.

Home of Helen Hayes. [Value of card: $3-5.]

Jean Hersholt (1886–1956)

Actor

Memorable Films: *The Four Horsemen of the Apocalypse* (1921); *The Country Doctor* (1936).

Jean Hersholt made his film debut in his native Denmark. After he came to America he distinguished himself in silent and sound films. Today, he is best known for the award that carries his name: The Jean Hersholt Humanitarian Award. The Academy of Motion Picture Arts and Sciences periodically awards it for outstanding contributions to humanitarian causes.

In the mid-1920s, Hersholt moved into a North Rodeo Drive house in Beverly Hills.

Jean Hersholt

Home of Jean Hersholt.
[Value of card: $8-10.]

Home of Jean Hersholt.
[Value of card: $3-5.]

Charlton Heston (1924–)

Actor

Memorable Films: *The Greatest Show on Earth* (1952); *The Ten Commandments* (1956).

Actor Charlton Heston has played both strong and unique roles on the screen. He is most famous for portraying Moses in *The Ten Commandments* (1958). But Heston has proven himself versatile in his art. As an astronaut in *Plant of the Apes* (1968) he winds up on a bizarre planet. Off-screen, Heston has served as president of the Screen Actors Guild.

Heston has lived in a home located in an area called Beverly Hills Post Office. Houses in this area have a Beverly Hills zip code but actually fall outside the city limits.

"Charlton Heston was twice the size of anyone I'd ever met. 'Impressive' is not an adequate description. He *was* Moses, Ben-Hur, Michelangelo—and God, all rolled into one."

—Screenwriter Norma Barzman

Home of Charlton Heston. [From postcard packet. Value of packet: $3-5.]

William Holden (1918–1981)

Actor

Memorable Films: *Golden Boy* (1939); *Network* (1976).

Few females get tired of looking at actor William Holden on the screen. Besides his good looks, the man could act and appeared in plenty of films. In 1981, Holden died after tripping on a rug in his home and hitting his head on a table.

South Driftwood Drive in Palm Springs was home to Holden for about a decade, beginning in the late 1960s.

William Holden

Home of William Holden. [Value of card: $3-5.]

Jack Holt (1888–1951)

Actor

Memorable Films: *The Little American* (1917); *North of the Rio Grande* (1922).

Actor Jack Holt appeared in nearly two-hundred films. He made it to leading man status. He was born in Virginia and was schooled at the Virginia Military Institute.

Jack Holt

Home of Jack Holt.
[Value of card: $3-5.]

Bob Hope (1903–2003)

Comedian/Actor

Memorable Films: *My Favorite Blonde* (1942); *The Paleface* (1948).

Entertainer Bob Hope could never have been president. That is because he was born in England in 1903. Still, he's considered an institution in America. Hope entertained via vaudeville, radio, film, books, and television. All these efforts, coupled with his investments, made Hope an extremely wealthy man. In 1973, *Playboy Magazine* asked Hope if he was indeed among the richest men in the world. "That's what they say," he replied, adding, "I wish somebody would tell me where all the money is."

Hope's primary home during his long career was in the Toluca Lake area of Los Angeles. He also bought two homes in Palm Springs in the 1940s. In 1979, architect John Lautner built Hope's famous domed mansion in Palm Springs.

Bob Hope

Home of Bob Hope. [Value of card: $3-5.]

Home of Bob Hope. [Value of card: $3-5.]

May Irwin (1862–1938)

Actress

Memorable Films: *The Kiss* (1896); *Mrs. Black Is Back* (1914).

Actress May Irwin made film history when she kissed John Rice in *The Kiss* (1896). It is the first kissing scene in cinematic history. The Broadway stage actress only appeared in one other film during her lifetime. Irwin owned a powerboat that was entered in the 1906 boat races held at the Frontenac Yacht Club at Thousand Islands, New York.

Home of May Irwin. [Value of card: $3-5.]

MAY IRWIN'S SUMMER HOME NEAR CLAYTON, THOUSAND ISLANDS, N.Y.

David Janssen (1931–1980)

Actor

Memorable Television Show: "The Fugitive" (1963–1967).

Television star David Janssen has appeared in *The Green Berets* (1968) and other films, but his work on television is far better known today. Janssen played Dr. Richard Kimble on the television series *The Fugitive*, which ran for several years in the 1960s. He was a graduate of Fairfax High School in Los Angeles.

Janssen spent much of his time in Palm Springs, enjoying the sun and casual lifestyle.

Palm Springs Home of
DAVID JANSSEN

Home of David Janssen. [Value of card: $3-5.]

Shirley Jones (1934–)

Actress
Memorable Film: *Elmer Gantry* (1960).
Memorable Television Show: "The Partridge Family" (1970–1974).

Shirley Jones is closely identified with her role as Shirley Partridge on television's "The Partridge Family." On film, she won an Oscar for Best Supporting Actress for her dramatic role in *Elmer Gantry* (1960).

Home of Shirley Jones. [From postcard packet. Value of packet: $3-5.]

Leatrice Joy (1893–1985)

Actress
Memorable Films: *Manslaughter* (1922); *The Ten Commandments* (1923).

Hollywood pioneer Cecil B. DeMille directed Leatrice Joy in many films. In researching her role for *Manslaughter* (1922), Joy toured the county jail in Los Angeles. After the actress lost her visitor's pass, a guard implied to Joy that she was in trouble and would have to be searched. Joy was relieved when she realized the guard had been playing a joke on her. Shortly before marrying Joy, actor John Gilbert said, "Whatever I may achieve in the future, or will ever be able to do,

I owe to Miss Joy," he said. The couple's two-year marriage ended in 1924.

A December 1926 "Society of Cinemaland" column in the *Los Angeles Times* noted an upcoming house-warming party. It was to be held by Joy at her new home in Beverly Hills.

Home of Leatrice Joy. [Value of card: $3-5.]

Buster Keaton (1895–1966)

Actor

Memorable Films: *Go West* (1925); *The Cameraman* (1928).

Buster Keaton

Buster Keaton once said the Beverly Hills Italian Villa mansion he built cost him "a lot of pratfalls." His dad, actor Joe Keaton, made him a stage favorite as a kid by physically tossing him around the stage while the audience roared with laughter. The younger Keaton would go on to perform plenty of physically challenging comedic feats as a silent star.

Keaton built his Italian Villa in the mid-1920s. The comic star's kids, James and Robert, so disliked having to wash up prior to meals, they once shut off all the valves to all faucets throughout their Beverly Hills mansion.

"I sometimes wonder if the world will ever seem as carefree and exciting a place as it did to us in Hollywood during 1919 and the early twenties. We were all young; the air in southern California was like wine. Our business was also young and growing like nothing ever seen."

—Buster Keaton

Home of Buster Keaton. [Value of card: $3-5.]

Home of Buster Keaton. [From postcard packet. Value of packet: $3-5.]

Frank Keenan (1858–1929)

Actor

Memorable Films: *The Bells of Asti* (1914); *Smoldering Embers* (1920).

Frank Keenan was a prominent stage actor before turning to film in the early years of moving pictures. His first silent films were released after he reached the age of fifty. One of his wives was stage actress Leah May.

**Home of Frank Keenan.
[Value of card: $3-5.]**

Grace Kelly (1929–1982)

Actress

Memorable Films: *Rear Window* (1954); *The Country Girl* (1954).

Actress Grace Kelly did not have to kiss a frog to become a princess. She just married Prince Rainier III of Monaco in 1956 and became one. Before she was ever called Princess Grace, she was famous for such films as *Mogambo* (1953) and *Rear Window* (1954). Kelly was also known for her on-screen beauty. Her friend, actress Ava Gardner, once addressed Kelly's looks. "If you saw her in a room," said Gardner, "she was rather plain. She photographed more beautifully than she actually was." An automobile accident cut Kelly's life short at the age of fifty-four.

The palace where Princess Kelly lived with Prince Rainier III in Monaco overlooks the Mediterranean Sea.

Grace Kelly

Home of Grace Kelly. [Value of card: $3-5.]

Norman Kerry (1894–1956)

Actor

Memorable Films: *The Hunchback of Notre Dame* (1923); *The Phantom of the Opera* (1925).

Actor Norman Kerry's trademark waxed mustaches served him well in silent films. Early in his career he appeared in films that starred big names. He appeared with Mary Pickford in *Amarilly of Clothes-Line Alley* (1918). Kerry was one of actor Rudolph Valentino's early Hollywood friends.

By the early 1920s, Kerry and his wife, Rosine, had a mansion on North Bedford Drive in Beverly Hills.

Norman Kerry

Home of Norman Kerry. [Value of card: $3-5.]

James Kirkwood (1875–1963) and Lila Lee (1901–1973)

Actor (Kirkwood) and Actress (Lee)

Memorable Films (James Kirkwood): *Home Sweet Home* (1914); *Bob Hampton of Placer* (1921).

Memorable Films (Lila Lee): *Blood and Sand* (1922); *The Unholy Three* (1930).

Stage and film actor James Kirkwood was a silent star who would also direct many films during the silent era. At the start of his career, he worked with the "Who's Who" of Hollywood pioneers, including director D.W. Griffith, actress Mary Pickford, and producer Mack Sennett. silent-star Lila Lee began acting in films as a teenager. Lee married and divorced the much-older Kirkwood in the 1920s.

Lila Lee

Home of James Kirkwood and Lila Lee. [Value of card: $3-5.]

Hedy Lamarr (1914–2000)

Actress

Memorable Films: *Ziegfeld Girl* (1941); *Samson and Delilah* (1949).

The drop-dead gorgeous Hedy Lamarr used her looks well in films. The actress made news in the mid-1960s, but it was not movie related. Lamarr was arrested for shoplifting.

Hedy Lamarr

Home of Hedy Lamarr.
[Value of card: $3-5.]

Burt Lancaster (1913–1994)

Actor

Memorable Films: *The Sweet Smell of Success* (1957); *Elmer Gantry* (1960).

The 1946 film, *The Killers,* was not only actor Burt Lancaster's first film, but a smashing success. His athletic prowess would serve him well in such films as *Jim Thorpe: All American* (1951) and *Trapeze* (1956). Lancaster married three times.

Home of Burt Lancaster.
[From postcard packet. Value of packet: $3-5.]

Rod La Roque (1898–1969) and Vilma Banky (1898–1991)

Actor (La Roque) and Actress (Banky)
Memorable Films (Rod La Roque): *The Ten Commandments* (1923); *Night Life of New York* (1925).
Memorable Films (Vilma Banky): *Son of the Sheik* (1926); *Two Lovers* (1928).

A popular silent star, actor Rod La Roque gained stage experience before tackling the silver screen. A versatile actor, he worked with big-name stars such as Marguerite Clark, Billie Burke, and Corinne Griffith. The star would marry actress Vilma Banky in 1927. Banky was born in Hungary in 1898 and became known to her fans as "The Hungarian Rhapsody." She came to Hollywood in the mid-1920s and would be teamed in films with leading man Ronald Colman. The marriage of Banky and La Roque lasted until La Roque's death in 1969.

Rod La Roque

Vilma Banky

MR. AND MRS. ROD LA ROCQUE HOME, (VILMA BANKY) 7056 LANEWOOD, HOLLYWOOD, CALIFORNIA   18

Home of Rod La Roque and Vilma Banky. [Value of card: $3-5.]

Ward Lascelle (1882–1941)

Producer

Memorable Films (as producer): *Affinities* (1922); *Western Grit* (1924).

Ward Lascelle had a brief Hollywood career as a producer and director of silent films in the 1920s. He produced some western films for cowboy actor Lester Cuneo. Lascelle directed actress Colleen Moore in a low-budget 1922 romantic-comedy film called *Affinities*.

Lascelle was thought to have lived in a Beverly Hills home that locals refer to as "The Witch's House." The Spadena House, as it is known in architectural circles, is on Walden Drive. Cartoonish,

Home of Ward Lascelle. [Value of card: $3-5.]

bizarre, and whimsical are words commonly used to describe the home. It was originally located in the Los Angeles suburb of Culver City prior to being moved to Beverly Hills.

Jesse Lasky (1880–1958)

Producer

Memorable Films (as producer): *The Covered Wagon* (1923); *The Adventures of Mark Twain* (1944).

Jesse Lasky was one of the early film moguls. He and Sam Goldwyn (then Samuel Goldfish) formed Jesse L. Lasky Feature Play Company. *The Squaw Man* (1914) was the first film the company produced. Through various business dealings, Jesse L. Lasky Feature Play Company lead to what today is Paramount Pictures.

Lasky had a home in Hollywood on Hillside Avenue. The producer would often ride a horse from the mansion to his Hollywood studio. Lasky had a Santa Monica

Home of Jesse Lasky. [Value of card: $3-5.]

beach house where he enjoyed the sand and water with his family.

"My father's hobby was amateur exploration. This might seem a bit unusual for a film mogul, a breed universally known to devote its spare time to gambling and philandering. Not that this benign, dignified, quiet-voiced gentleman who presided so enthusiastically at our family occasions like Christmas, Thanksgiving, and birthday dinners was above the more addictive pursuits of happiness."

—Screenwriter Jesse Lasky, Jr.

Home of Jesse Lasky.
[Value of card: $3-5.]

Chester Lauck (1902–1980) and Norris Goff (1906–1978)

Radio Actors

Memorable Radio Show (Chester Lauck and Norris Goff): "Lum 'N' Abner" (1931–1953).

Chester Lauck and Norris Goff were a famous radio acting duo. They played two old-time philosophers from Arkansas named Columbus "Lum" Edwards (Lauck) and Abner Peabody (Goff) on the "Lum 'N' Abner" radio program. Lauck and Goff met each other as kids while attending a birthday party.

Both Lauck and Goff lived in Mena, Arkansas.

"It was situation comedy. And that's the reason these old shows are playing so well today, because they're not jokes—they're just situations that will always be funny and timeless."

—Chester Lauck describing the "Lum 'N' Abner" radio show

Chester Lauck (Lum) and Norris Goff (Abner)

Homes of Chester Lauck and Norris Goff. [Value of card: $4-6.]

Home of Norris Goff (Abner). [Value of card: $4-6.]

Jack Lemmon (1925–2001)

Actor

Memorable Films: *Some Like It Hot* (1959); *The Apartment* (1960).

Jack Lemmon first went in front of a camera as an actor in the late 1940s, working mainly on television. His early film successes included the 1955 comedy-film *Mr. Roberts*. One of his most celebrated roles, in the movie *Some Like It Hot* (1959), garnered Lemon an Oscar for Best Actor in a Leading Role.

In the early 1960s, Lemmon and his wife, Felicia, purchased a French provincial mansion in Beverly Hills.

Home of Jack Lemmon. [From postcard packet. Value of packet: $3-5.]

84

Jerry Lewis (1926–)

Comedian/Actor

Memorable Films: *The Nutty Professor* (1963); *King of Comedy* (1983).

The famous comedy team of Dean Martin and Jerry Lewis were a hit on film and as a nightclub act. But they are almost as famous for their split in the mid-1950s. Martin and Lewis began to heal their rift in 1976. By 1989, Lewis was heard telling Dean, "Why we broke up, I'll never know."

In the 1950s, Lewis was named honorary mayor of Pacific Palisades, the Los Angeles community where he lived.

ome of Jerry Lewis, Pacific Palisades, California

Home of Jerry Lewis. [From postcard packet. Value of packet: $3-5.]

Home of Jerry Lewis. [From postcard packet. Value of packet: $3-5.]

Home of Jerry Lewis. [Value of card: $3-5.]

Liberace (1919–1987)

Musician
Memorable Television Show: "The Liberace Show" (1952–1955).

Pianist Liberace became a star in the 1950s and would come to be known as "Mr. Show-manship." He earned the title by dazzling audiences with his piano playing, fancy clothes, and stage props. In late 1963, doctors feared that Liberace was dying of uremic poisoning. His doctor suggested he plan his final affairs. Liberace contacted his accountant to figure out how much he was worth. The answer he got was $750,000.

In the 1950s, Liberace moved into a Sherman Oaks house that featured a piano-shaped pool. He started enjoying a second home in Palm Springs as well. He initially named his last Palm Springs home "The Cloisters." He would later rename it "Casa de Liberace." He died at the home in 1987.

"I'm no good—I've just got guts."
—Liberace

Home of Liberace. [Value of card: $3-5.]

Home of Liberace. [Value
of card: $3-5.]

Home of Liberace.
[Value of card: $3-5.]

Home of Liberace.
[Value of card: $3-5.]

Home of Liberace. [From postcard packet. Value of packet: $3-5.]

Home of Liberace. [From postcard packet. Value of packet: $3-5.]

Harold Lloyd (1893–1971)

Actor

Memorable Films: *Safety Last* (1923); *Girl Shy* (1924).

While less well-known than peers Charles Chaplin and Buster Keaton, actor Harold Lloyd is still considered a giant in comedy films of the silent era. He did not hide from his days as a silent star in retirement. In his later years, Lloyd loved nothing more than to chat about his silent-screen days.

Lloyd had a Los Angeles home on South Irving Boulevard before building a mansion in Beverly Hills in the late 1920s. The Italian-Renaissance mansion on Benedict Canyon Drive was named Greenacres. Although the mansion contained dozens of rooms and fancy furnishings, Lloyd's wife, Mildred, once confessed that the elevator "was the only cozy place in the house."

Harold Lloyd

Greenacres, the home of Harold Lloyd. [Value of card: $3-5.]

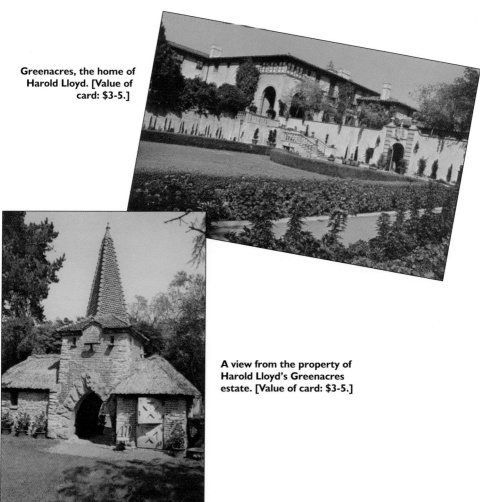

A view from the property of Harold Lloyd's Greenacres estate. [Value of card: $3-5.]

A view from the property of Harold Lloyd's Greenacres estate. [Value of card: $3-5.]

A view from the property of Harold Lloyd's Greenacres estate. [Value of card: $3-5.]

Home of Harold Lloyd. [Value of card: $3-5.]

A view from the property of Harold Lloyd's Greenacres estate. [Value of card: $3-5.]

Carole Lombard (1908–1942)

Actress

Memorable Films: *The Twentieth Century* (1934); *My Man Godfrey* (1936).

Carole Lombard's acting career started during the 1920s, but she became a big star in the 1930s. Lombard would marry actor William Powell, divorce him, and then claim another famous husband, actor Clark Gable. Tragedy struck in 1942 when Lombard died in a plane crash at the age of thirty-three. "I am so unbelievably shocked that I don't know what to say," Powell said at the time.

Carole Lombard at home. [Value of card: $3-5.]

"My wife and I have been up all night waiting for reports. Our deepest sympathy goes to Clark Gable and Carole's two brothers."

Home of Carole Lombard. [Value of card: $3-5.]

Edmund Lowe (1890–1971)

Actor

Memorable Films: *What Price Glory?* (1926); *The Cisco Kid* (1931).

Edmund Lowe

Actor Edmund Lowe began what would become a one-hundred-plus film career during the silent era. He was a quick study in college, earning his Bachelor of Arts degree from the University of Santa Clara when he was eighteen years old, followed by a Master's degree at age nineteen. Shortly after the actor's death in April 1971, The Silent Movie Theater in Los Angeles announced that it would screen the 1924 film, *Barbara Frietchie,* as a tribute to Lowe, who starred in it.

In the mid-1920s, Lowe began living on North Linden Drive in Beverly Hills.

Home of Edmund Lowe. [From postcard packet. Value of packet: $3-5.]

Myrna Loy (1905–1993)

Actress

Memorable Films: *The Thin Man* (1934); *The Best Years of Our Lives* (1946).

During the silent era, actress Myrna Loy played a vamp. Talking pictures brought her more lady-like roles. Loy is best known for *The Thin Man* movie series, in which she played opposite William Powell. Loy once admitted to being terrible with finances. Marriage was not one of her strong points either. Loy was married and divorced four times.

Early in her career, Loy lived in Beverly Hills, with her mother, on North Crescent Drive starting in the mid-1920s.

Home of Myrna Loy. [Value of card: $4-6.]

Loretta Lynn (1932–)

Singer

Memorable Songs: "Don't Come Home a Drinkin' (With Lovin' on Your Mind)" (1966); "After the Fire is Gone" (1971).

Country-music star Loretta Lynn began singing at school gatherings as a teen. Her debut single, "I'm a Honky Tonk Girl," was released in 1960. Lynn has been a high achiever, despite making it only to the eighth grade. "You don't need book learnin' to have good horse sense," Lynn once said.

Lynn was raised on a farm in Butcher Holler, Kentucky. Her ranch is called Loretta Lynn's Ranch. It is located in Hurricane Mills, Tennessee, and is a popular tourist attraction. Lynn's ranch offers cabin rentals and paddle boats.

Childhood home of Loretta Lynn. [Value of card: $3-5.]

Home of Loretta Lynn

Home of Loretta Lynn. [Value of card: $3-5.]

Jeanette MacDonald (1903–1965)

Singer/Actress
Memorable Films: *Naughty Marietta* (1935); *San Francisco* (1936).

A singer on stage and in film, Jeanette MacDonald was an MGM darling in the 1930s. MacDonald's movie career was relatively brief, ending in the late 1940s. Until she became a star, the actress didn't appreciate the impact that movie stardom had on the average person. "I never realized how much movie stars mean to people," said MacDonald. "It makes you feel embarrassed and rather humble and happy all at once."

Jeanette MacDonald

Home of Jeanette MacDonald. [Value of card: $3-5.]

Jeanette MacDonald (1903–1965) and Gene Raymond (1908–1988)

Singer/Actress (MacDonald) and Actor (Raymond)
Memorable Films (Jeanette MacDonald): *Naughty Marietta* (1935); *San Francisco* (1936).
Memorable Films (Gene Raymond): *Red Dust* (1932); *Mr. and Mrs. Smith* (1941).

Jeanette MacDonald took her soprano voice to Broadway and film and became a star. The pretty actress would marry actor Gene Raymond in the late 1930s. He landed a film contract with Paramount Pictures, which released his first film, *Personal Maid*, in 1931. The couple's marriage lasted until MacDonald's death in 1965.

After marrying in 1937, MacDonald and Raymond moved into a mansion called Twin Gables. The home, located in Bel-Air, a community near Beverly Hills, was a gift from Raymond to his new bride.

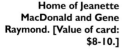

Home of Jeanette MacDonald and Gene Raymond. [Value of card: $8-10.]

Douglas MacLean (1890–1967)

Actor

Memorable Films: *The Hun Within* (1918); *Divorce Made Easy* (1929).

Actor Douglas MacLean performed on Broadway with actress Maude Adams in *Peter Pan*. He also acted in and produced silent films. *Hold That Lion* (1926) and *Let it Rain* (1927) were made by Douglas MacLean Productions.

MacLean lived in at least three Beverly Hills homes.

Douglas MacLean

Home of Douglas MacLean. [From postcard packet. Value of packet: $3-5.]

Fred MacMurray (1908–1991)

Actor

Memorable Film: *Double Indemnity* (1944).

Memorable Television Show: "My Three Sons" (1960–1972).

Fred MacMurray could never be accused of acting before a camera. His characters came across on screen so convincing that you could be fooled into believing they would still be there after the cameras stopped rolling. It is certainly not fair to his long career, but MacMurray has two overriding legacies: television's "My Three Sons" and the 1944 film, *Double Indemnity*.

MacMurray had a home in the Los Angeles community of Brentwood.

Fred MacMurray

Home of Fred MacMurray. [Value of card: $8-10.]

Fredric March (1887–1975)

Actor

Memorable Films: *A Star Is Born* (1937); *The Best Years of Our Lives* (1946).

During the heyday of the Hollywood studio system, actor Fredric March was happy not being anchored for long to any one studio. Off-screen, he did enjoy being tied to someone. March was married to actress Florence Eldridge for decades, until his passing in 1975. The couple married in 1927.

March built his Beverly Hills mansion in the 1930s on Ridgedale Drive. His wife, Florence, said March "seemed to enjoy all our nests." The Normandy-style mansion was designed by architect Wallace Neff.

Fredric March

Home of Fredric March. [Value of card: $3-5.]

Dean Martin (1917–1995)

Singer/Actor

Memorable Film: *Rio Bravo* (1959).

Memorable Song: "You're Nobody Til Somebody Loves You" (1964).

Dean Martin was one-half of one of the most successful comedic pairings in entertainment history. His partner was entertainer Jerry Lewis. The two performed on stage and in films such as *Scared Stiff* (1953). Ricci Martin, Dean Martin's son, recalled an incident that could have come straight out of a Martin and Lewis movie. "One night, he took Mom to dinner at Chasen's and they drove his Rolls Royce. After dinner, they came home and parked in the garage, and just as Dad was coming into the house he turned around and looked at the Rolls with puzzlement. It wasn't his car. The valet at Chasen's had given Dad the wrong Rolls Royce to drive home," Ricci explained.

Martin had a home in Beverly Hills on Mountain Drive where he raised his kids. He spent many years enjoying a second home in Palm Springs. It was located in the Las Palmas neighborhood on Via Monte Vista.

Home of Dean Martin. [From postcard packet. Value of packet: $3-5.]

Home of Dean Martin. [Value of card: $3-5.]

96

Mary Martin (1913–1990)

Singer/Actress

Memorable Broadway Stage Performance: *South Pacific* (1949).

Singer Mary Martin performed on the Broadway stage, film, and television. Martin loved playing to a live audience. "Give me four people and I'm *on*," stated Martin. "Give me four-hundred and I'm a hundred times more on." Martin is the mother of actor Larry Hagman. Her death in 1990 was front-page news in *The New York Times*.

Martin lived in Weatherford, Texas, as a child.

Mary Martin

Childhood home of Mary Martin. [Value of card: $3-5.]

Tony Martin (1912–)

Singer/Actor

Memorable Films: *Ziegfeld Girl* (1941); *Here Come the Girls* (1953).

Actor Tony Martin used his vocal talents to become a Hollywood star. The singer has made a lot of nightclub appearances during his long entertainment career. He married actress Alice Faye in the late 1930s, but they would divorce in 1940. Martin has been married to dancer Cyd Charisse since the late 1940s.

Martin and his wife, Cyd, have been closely associated with the Palm Springs area for many years.

Home of Tony Martin. [Value of card: $3-5.]

Groucho Marx (1890–1977)

Actor

Memorable Films: *Cocoanuts* (1929); *A Night at the Opera* (1935).

For fans of Groucho Marx, there is no better comic performer. His humor and delivery style remain one of a kind. Marx and his brothers formed a comedy team called the Marx Brothers and starred in several hit movies that continue to be audience favorites. As leader of this band of laughs, Marx played a cigar smoking, smarty-pants who had a stooped walk and a big mustache. According to his son, Arthur, Marx hated Hollywood's "ostentatious living, the false adulation—in fact, the whole social scheme as reported in the fan

Home of Groucho Marx. [From postcard packet. Value of packet: $3-5.]

magazines." So, when Marx finally purchased a mansion in Beverly Hills in the late 1930s, he had mixed feelings. "I fought this off as long as I could but here I am, just another yokel," Marx wrote to a friend.

Marx bought a mansion on North Foothill Road in Beverly Hills in the 1940s. During the later years of his life, he lived in the Trousdale Estates area of Beverly Hills.

Home of Groucho Marx. [From postcard packet. Value of packet: $3-5.]

May McAvoy (1899–1984)

Actress

Memorable Films: *The Enchanted Cottage* (1924); *Ben-Hur* (1925).

New York native May McAvoy was a silent-screen star who worked with many early Hollywood greats, including actors Marguerite Clark, Lionel Barrymore, and Wallace Reid. During that period, McAvoy formed a meeting group for young actresses. It was called Our Club. She was the 1923 Rose Queen of the Pasadena Tournament of Roses. McAvoy worked with director Ernst Lubitsch who apparently had trouble with her name. "He always pronounced it McAwoy," recalled the star.

Home of May McAvoy. [Value of card: $3-5.]

John McCormick (1893–1961) and Colleen Moore (1900–1988)

Producer (McCormick) and Actress (Moore)
Memorable Films (John McCormick, as producer): *Ella Cinders* (1926); *Lilac Time* (1928).
Memorable Films (Colleen Moore): *Flaming Youth* (1923); *Lilac Time* (1928).

John McCormick produced many Colleen Moore movies. The two married in 1923 and divorced in 1930. Moore was a child when she decided she wanted to act. Her films still play at special movie house showings.

Moore bought a mansion in Bel-Air, a Los Angeles community, while still married to McCormick. "The house had so many rooms I'm not sure I ever saw them all," Moore once said.

Colleen Moore

Colleen Moore

RESIDENCE OF MR. AND MRS. JOHN McCORMICK, (COLLEEN MOORE), BEVERLY HILLS

Home of John McCormick and Colleen Moore. [From postcard packet. Value of packet: $3-5.]

Victor McLaglen (1883–1959)

Actor

Memorable Films: *The Beloved Brute* (1924); *The Quiet Man* (1952).

Victor McLaglen was not playing a role when he was a prizefighter in Canada. He would eventually turn to a less physically demanding career for money, acting. The British-born McLaglen started acting in silent films in Britain. He would make it to Hollywood and won an Oscar for Best Actor in a Leading Role for *The Informer* (1935).

McLaglen was living in Beverly Hills in the mid-1920s.

Victor McLaglen

Home of Victor McLaglen. [Value of card: $3-5.]

Ed McMahon (1923–)

Television Personality

Memorable Television Show: "The Tonight Show Starring Johnny Carson" (1962–1992).

Ed McMahon was the straight-man for Johnny Carson on Carson's television show. McMahon was on "The Tonight Show Starring Johnny Carson" for its entire thirty-year run which began in the early 1960s.

Home of Ed McMahon. [From postcard packet. Value of packet: $3-5.]

Steve McQueen (1930–1980)

Actor

Memorable Films: *The Great Escape* (1963); *Papillon* (1973).

Steve McQueen made a successful, high-paying career out of being the coolest guy on the screen. He could also be cool at calculating the odds of improving his chances for success. "I'm glad Dean's dead," McQueen once told writer John Gilmore not more than a year after actor James Dean's death in 1956. "It makes more room for me."

McQueen called Los Angeles, Malibu, and Palm Springs home during his career.

Home of Steve McQueen.
[Value of card: $3-5.]

Thomas Meighan (1879–1936)

Actor

Memorable Films: *The Miracle Man* (1919); *The Alaskan* (1924).

Six-foot actor Thomas Meighan first acted on stage in his home town of Pittsburgh, Pennsylvania. Meighan would act in over seventy-five films.

Meighan built a winter vacation home in New Port Richey, Florida, in the late 1920s. *New Port Richey Press* reported on June 25, 1926, "New Port Richey's beautiful new motion picture theatre has been named the 'Thomas Meighan Theatre' in tribute to the famous film star who has adopted New Port Richey as his favorite Florida city."

Thomas Meighan

Home of Thomas Meighan. [Value of card: $4-6.]

Patsy Ruth Miller (1904–1995)

Actress

Memorable Films: *Camille* (1921); *The Hunchback of Notre Dame* (1923).

Brown-eyed actress Patsy Ruth Miller rose to film stardom in the early 1920s. Charles Ray, Cullen Landis, Tom Mix, and Hoot Gibson were among her on-screen lovers. "Really, I can't tell you anything about love!" said Miller in 1923. "I've been so busy making love in pictures I haven't had time to find out what it's all about in real life."

A December 1926 column in the *Los Angeles Times* called "Society of Cinemaland" spoke of an upcoming party at Miller's Beverly Hills home. The gathering was to take place on the day after Christmas. The article noted that one of the guests of honor was to be Donald Freeman, editor of *Vogue* and *Vanity Fair*.

Patsy Ruth Miller

Home of Patsy Ruth Miller.
[Value of card: $3-5.]

Tom Mix (1880–1940)

Actor

Memorable Films: *Ranch Life in the Great Southwest* (1910); *Riders of the Purple Sage* (1925).

Tom Mix was a cowboy star during the silent era. The actor's sidekick was his horse, Tony. In 1919, Mix was asked why a member of his film company would be proud of being thrown in jail for horse theft. "Well, I dunno, mebbe [sic] he stole a good hoss [sic]!" Mix offered.

In the 1920s, Mix moved into a Beverly Hills mansion on Summit Drive. Inside, the home resembled a museum dedicated to Mix's ego. Silver-embossed saddles, guns, and trophies where laid out in one of the rooms. Outside, a neon sign with Mix's initials sat atop the roof.

Tom Mix

Home of Tom Mix. [From postcard packet. Value of packet: $3-5.]

Home of Tom Mix. [Value of card: $3-5.]

Marilyn Monroe (1926–1962)

Actress

Memorable Films: *Seven Year Itch* (1955); *The Misfits* (1961).

    Actress Marilyn Monroe is more of a legend than a movie star. Her face continues to be recognizable to almost anybody of any age, even though she died four decades ago. The sexy blonde star had a difficult life. And, by some accounts, she wanted out of it badly enough to end it herself. Monroe last starred in the John Huston-directed film *The Misfits* (1961). It was filmed in Nevada. During a break in the filming Huston hosted a party and ended up at a barroom crap table with Monroe. Before rolling the dice, Monroe asked Huston, "What should I ask the dice for John?" Huston told Monroe, "Don't think honey, just throw. That's the story of your life. Don't think—do it."

    Monroe lived in Beverly Hills during her marriage to baseball great Joe DiMaggio in the 1950s.

Home of Marilyn Monroe. [From postcard packet. Value of packet: $3-5.]

Home of Marilyn Monroe. [Value of card: $7-9.]

Robert Montgomery (1904–1981)

Actor

Memorable Films: *Mr. and Mrs. Smith* (1941); *Here Comes Mr. Jordan* (1941).

Actor Robert Montgomery was paired on film with big names such as Norma Shearer and Joan Crawford. Montgomery later gained fame for his television series, "Robert Montgomery Presents," which ran for many years in the 1950s. His daughter was Elizabeth Montgomery, the star of "Bewitched," the television series that began in the 1960s.

Robert Montgomery

Home of Robert Montgomery. [Value of card: $3-5.]

Home of Robert Montgomery. [Value of card: $3-5.]

Colleen Moore (1900–1988)

Actress

Memorable Films: *Flaming Youth* (1923); *Lilac Time* (1928).

Cuteness, coupled with brown hair and acting skills, propelled Colleen Moore to silent-star fame. The actress worked with such directors as William Seiter and Marshall Neilan. But Moore said that Charles Brabin "was the director who could get the most out of me." He directed her in *Twinkletoes* (1926).

Colleen Moore

Coleen Moore

565-2

RESIDENCE OF COLLEEN MOORE, LOS ANGELES, CALIFORNIA

Home of Colleen Moore. [Value of card: $3-5.]

Tom Moore (1883–1955)

Actor

Memorable Films: *Manhandled* (1924); *The Last Parade* (1931).

Born in Ireland, actor Tom Moore starred in and directed many silent films. His brother was actor Owen Moore, who was once married to silent-star Mary Pickford. Moore's Hollywood career would span over four decades, ending shortly before his death in 1955. His wife, Elinor Merry, said Moore was brave in facing death at the hands of cancer. He also kept his sense of humor. She said Moore's last words were: "I certainly will know how to play a death scene after *this.*"

Tom Moore

Home of Tom Moore. [Value of card: $3-5.]

Antonio Moreno (1887–1967)

Actor

Memorable Films: *The Temptress* (1926); *The Searchers* (1955).

Antonio Moreno was one of the most famous Latin-lovers on the silent-screen. Though his career peaked in the 1920s, he would continue to act for decades. As a boy working in his native Spain, he was asked his name by a couple of American tourists. "Antonio Garida Moreno Montagudo, at the service of you and God," the young boy responded. This so impressed the tourists that they arranged for Moreno to be brought to New York for schooling. Despite some financial set backs in real estate development, Moreno died wealthy in 1967, at the age of eighty.

Antonio Moreno at home. [From postcard packet. Value of packet: $4-6.]

Over the years, Moreno's 1920s mansion has been called Crestmont, The Paramour, and Canfield-Moreno Estate. It was built by his father-in-law, Charles Canfield, and sits west of the Silver Lake Reservoir in Los Angeles.

Home of Antonio Moreno. [Value of card: $4-6.]

Home of Antonio Moreno. [Value of card: $4-6.]

Charles Murray (1872–1941)

Actor

Memorable Films: *Mike* (1926); *Lost at the Front* (1927).

By the sheer number of films he appeared in (250-plus), actor Charles Murray's career is impressive. His early screen appearances were for the Biograph Company. Producer Mack Sennett would employ him for many years.

CHARLES MURRAY'S HOME, HOLLYWOOD, CALIFORNIA 22

Home of Charles Murray. [Value of card: $3-5.]

Conrad Nagel (1897–1970)

Actor

Memorable Films: *Little Women* (1919); *Tess of the D'Urbervilles* (1924).

Conrad Nagel was a silent player who was said to project a less-than-remarkable image on film. Silent-film historian Anthony Slide called Nagel a "bland performer." Still, he had an acting career that began in 1918 and spanned decades.

Nagel is counted among the first batch of silent stars who were early residents of Beverly Hills.

Conrad Nagel

812A:—Conrad Nagel's Home, Beverly Hills, Calif.

**Home of Conrad Nagel.
[Value of card: $3-5.]**

Alla Nazimova (1879–1945)

Actress

Memorable Films: *Camille* (1921); *Salome* (1923).

Actress Alla Nazimova was born in Russia and played violin as a child. She started her acting career on the stage in Moscow at the Artistic Theater. Nazimova came to America after the turn of the century with a Russian theater company to do stage work. She would make her way onto the silent screen with films such as *Toys of Fate* (1918).

Home of Alla Nazimova. [Value of card: $4-6.]

Nazimova bought a mansion on Sunset Boulevard while she was still acting in silent films.

Pola Negri (1894–1987)

Actress

Memorable Films: *Passion* (1919); *Forbidden Paradise* (1924).

Polish-born actress Pola Negri was a silent star known for her off-screen melodramatic behavior and romances. Among Negri's famous boyfriends were actors Rudolph Valentino and Charles Chaplin. She performed a vamp-type role in *Bella Donna* (1923). Actress Theda Bara commented late in life about Negri's vamp image. "Pola Negri copied *me*," Bara said when insisting she, not Negri, was the first movie vamp.

Pola Negri

Home of Pola Negri. [Value of card: $3-5.]

Home of Pola Negri.
[Value of card: $3-5.]

Pola Negri at home. [Value of card: $3-5.]

Home of Pola Negri.
[From postcard
packet. Value of
packet: $3-5.]

Paul Newman (1925–)

Actor

Memorable Films: *Hombre* (1967); *Butch Cassidy and the Sundance Kid* (1969).

The acting talents of Paul Newman have, at times, been overshadowed by his good looks. Newman also has a beautiful wife, actress Joanne Woodward, who he married in the late 1950s. The actor's secret for maintaining a long marriage with Woodward? "Why go out for hamburger when you have steak at home," Newman explained.

Newman lived in more than one home in the city of Beverly Hills during his long movie career.

Home of Paul Newman. [From postcard packet. Value of packet: $3-5.]

Fred Niblo (1874–1948)

Director

Memorable Films (as Director): *Blood and Sand* (1922); *Ben-Hur* (1927).

Fred Niblo was a silent-film director. He did some film acting and producing as well. Niblo married actress Enid Bennett as her film career was getting under way. He directed Bennett in films such as *The Woman in the Suitcase* (1920) and *Silk Hosiery* (1920).

Niblo lived in Beverly Hills during his Hollywood days.

Home of Fred Niblo. [Value of card: $3-5.]

RESIDENCE OF FRED NIBLO, BEVERLY HILLS, CALIFORNIA

Mabel Normand (1895–1930)

Actress

Memorable Films: *Tillie's Punctured Romance* (1914); *Mickey* (1918).

"I never hold a grudge," actress Mabel Normand told a reporter in the 1920s. "Life is too short." Life was short for silent-star Normand, who died in 1930 at age thirty-four. She was known to party heavily and abuse drugs and alcohol. Today, Normand is all but forgotten. But when she made films for producer Mack Sennett, Normand was extremely popular with screen audiences.

In the 1920s, Normand moved into a North Camden Drive home in Beverly Hills.

Home of Mabel Normand. [Value of card: $25-50.]

Kim Novak (1933–)

Actress

Memorable Films: *The Man With the Golden Arm* (1955); *Strangers When We Meet* (1960).

Blonde-bombshell actress Kim Novak plunged into Hollywood in the mid-1950s. She starred opposite William Holden in the 1955 film, *Picnic*. There were rumors in the late 1950s that Novak and singer Sammy Davis, Jr. were romantically involved.

Home of Kim Novak. [Value of card: $3-5.]

Jack Oakie (1903–1978)

Actor

Memorable Films: *Million Dollar Legs* (1932); *The Great Dictator* (1940).

Jack Oakie began his stage and film acting in the early 1920s, but would bank most of his film work in the 1930s and 1940s. Oakie wrapped up his career with television work. In the late 1950s he appeared on "The Real McCoys" and in the mid-1960s he was seen on "Bonanza."

Oakie lived in a North Elm Drive home in Beverly Hills.

Home of Jack Oakie. [Value of card: $8-10.]

Wheeler Oakman (1890–1949) and Priscilla Dean (1896–1987)

Actor (Oakman) and Actress (Dean)

Memorable Films (Wheeler Oakman): *Mickey* (1918); *Lights of New York* (1928).

Memorable Films (Priscilla Dean): *Outside the Law* (1920); *The Dice Woman* (1926).

Actor Wheeler Oakman played many western parts in his film career. He played Dick Randall in the western film called *Revenge* (1918). But Oakman was not strictly a western actor by any means. He played in the drama *Bank Alarm* (1938).

Actress Priscilla Dean would marry Oakman in 1920. The two appeared opposite each other in the 1920 film, *The Virgin of Stamboul*. Oakman was able to make the transition to talkies and continued acting until shortly before his death in the late 1940s. Dean exited films in the early 1930s.

Priscilla Dean

Home of Wheeler Oakman and Priscilla Dean. [Value of card: $3-5.]

Eugene O'Brien (1880–1966)

Actor

Memorable Films: *The Moonstone* (1915); *The Wonderful Change* (1920).

A handsome six footer with blue eyes, Eugene O'Brien was put under contract by theatrical producer Charles Frohman before appearing on the silver screen. He became a leading man in films, working with the likes of Mary Pickford and Marguerite Clark. O'Brien's Hollywood career would begin and end in the silent-film era.

Home of Eugene O'Brien.
[Value of card: $10-12.]

Pat O'Brien (1899–1983)

Actor

Memorable Films: *Angels with Dirty Faces* (1938); *The Fighting 69th* (1940).

Pat O'Brien began his acting career in the early 1930s. O'Brien, who often co-starred with his friend, James Cagney, played a pivotal role of Father Jerry Connelly in the Cagney film, *Angels with Dirty Faces* (1938). From the early 1950s until the end of his career in the 1980s, O'Brien appeared mostly on television.

Home of Pat O'Brien. [Value of card: $3-5.]

Edna May Oliver (1883–1942)

Actress

Memorable Films: *Little Women* (1933); *Drums Along the Mohawk* (1939).

Edna May Oliver acted on Broadway with the future Hollywood icons like Marion Davies. In silent films she worked with stars such as Richard Dix and Bebe Daniels. During much of her career, Oliver rotated her Broadway work with her film appearances.

Home of Edna May Oliver.
[From postcard packet.
Value of packet: $3-5.]

Patti Page (1927–)

Singer

Memorable Songs: "Tennessee Waltz" (1950); "Old Cape Cod" (1957).

Patti Page got her start on radio as a singer in the 1940s. She would sing with the Jimmy Joy band and then begin recording her own records in the late 1940s. During the 1950s she recorded a number of hits, such as "Detour" (1951), and "Old Cape Cod" (1957).

A Cape Cod-style mansion in Beverly Hills was home at one time for Page. By the mid-1970s, the Hollywood couple Robert Wagner and Natalie Wood was living at the North Canon Drive property.

Home of Patti Page.
[From postcard
packet. Value of
packet: $3-5.]

Jack Palance (1919–2006)

Actor

Memorable Films: *Shane* (1953); *City Slickers* (1991).

Actor Jack Palance played the gun-slinging, all-around bad dude, Jack Wilson, in the movie *Shane* (1953). In the movie his rival Shane, played by Alan Ladd, tells Wilson he has heard that he was "a low-down Yankee liar!" Wilson responds with, "Prove it!" Shane does prove it with better gunmanship. But Palance, once again, had proven something too: he was a skilled actor. He didn't always care for the directors he worked with in film. "Most of them shouldn't even be directing traffic," Palance once said.

Home of Jack Palance. [From postcard packet. Value of packet: $3-5.]

Palance lived in Beverly Hills, on a corner lot, for decades.

Gregory Peck (1916–2003)

Actor

Memorable Films: *The Man in the Gray Flannel Suit* (1956); *To Kill a Mockingbird* (1963).

Actor Gregory Peck was a tall, well-groomed leading-man. Nothing but good traits—kindness, smarts, character—come to mind when Peck's name is mentioned. When the cameras were not rolling, he was active in political and humanitarian causes. Such interests matched Peck's screen image.

Beginning in the 1950s, Peck made Brentwood, a community in Los Angeles, his home.

Gregory Peck

Home of Gregory Peck. [From postcard packet. Value of packet: $3-5.]

117

Dorothy Phillips (1882–1980)

Actress

Memorable Films: *The Heart of Humanity* (1919); *The Postman Always Rings Twice* (1946).

Starting with her first role in 1911, actress Dorothy Phillips appeared in films for decades. She was famous enough as a silent star to be featured in a 1920 reference book, *Who's Who on the Screen*. She died in 1980, largely forgotten by the public.

823:—Dorothy Phillips and Her Home, Los Angeles, Calif.

Dorothy Phillips at home. [Value of card: $3-5.]

Mary Pickford (1892–1979)

Actress

Memorable Films: *Rebecca of Sunnybrook Farm* (1917); *Sparrows* (1926).

Mary Pickford was a famous silent star. She married actor Douglas Fairbanks in 1920. The couple lived in a famous Beverly Hills mansion called Pickfair. Pickford's close friends included actress Lillian Gish and screenwriter Frances Marion. Actress May McAvoy said of Pickford, "She was very lonely." McAvoy described Pickford as a prisoner of Pickfair while she lived there with Fairbanks.

Before Pickford married Fairbanks, she rented a Los Angeles mansion in a gated community.

Mary Pickford

Mary Pickford's Residence, Los Angeles, Cal.

Home of Mary Pickford. [Value of card: $7-9.]

MARY PICKFORD'S BIRTHPLACE, TORONTO, ONTARIO—12

Birthplace of Mary Pickford. [Value of card: $3-5.]

Webb Pierce (1921–1991)

Singer

Memorable Songs: "Wondering" (1952); "Slowly" (1954).

Webb Pierce's nasal singing voice didn't stop him from becoming a hugely successful honky-tonk singer and musician, especially in the 1950s and early 1960s. His 1954 song, "Slowly," is credited by many for introducing the pedal steel guitar to country music.

Pierce had a mansion in Oak Hill (part of Metropolitan Nashville), Tennessee, that was famous for its guitar-shaped pool. Singer Ray Stevens, a neighbor, organized a successful legal campaign to stop the tour buses from driving by the Pierce home. Stevens did not like the buses in his neighborhood. "That's what he gets for livin' across the street from a star," Pierce joked.

"I've been blessed with so much. I guess it turned out the way I wanted it."

—Webb Pierce

Webb Pierce at home. [Value of card: $3-5.]

Lily Pons (1898–1976)

Singer

Memorable Film: *I Dream Too Much* (1935).

Memorable Performance: Metropolitan Opera (1931).

French-born Lily Pons was a famous opera singer who made her first appearance at the Metropolitan Opera in New York in the early 1930s. Pons had a coloratura-soprano voice. She would also appear in a few movies during her entertainment career.

In the mid-1950s, Pons began enjoying the sunshine of Palm Springs while living on Cahuilla Hills Drive.

Home of Lily Pons. [Value of card: $3-5.]

Dick Powell (1904–1963)

Actor

Memorable Films: *Gold Diggers of 1937* (1936); *Murder, My Sweet* (1944).

Powell would put food on the table by singing before he turned to acting. The Arkansas-born Powell teamed with actress Joan Blondell in musicals such as *Stage Struck* (1936). Powell and Blondell married in 1936. He would become wealthy from both his Hollywood earnings and real estate investments.

Powell lived in the Los Angeles community of Toluca Lake at one point in his career.

Dick Powell

Home of Dick Powell. [From postcard packet. Value of packet: $3-5.]

William Powell (1892–1984)

Actor

Memorable Films: *The Thin Man* (1934); *My Man Godfrey* (1936).

The best career move actor William Powell made was to team with actress Myrna Loy to make *The Thin Man* (1934). The mystery-coupled-with-comedy film became a movie series and propelled him to stardom. Among Powell's off-screen lovers was actress Jean Harlow. He married and divorced actress Carole Lombard in the early 1930s.

William Powell

Home of William Powell. [Value of card: $4-6.]

Tyrone Power (1914–1958)

Actor

Memorable Films: *In Old Chicago* (1937); *Witness for the Prosecution* (1956).

A romantic actor and busy leading-man, Tyrone Power was the son of silent-film actor Tyrone Power Sr. Power was married to actresses Linda Christian and Annabella. Neither marriage would last.

Home of Tyrone Power.
[Value of card: $3-5.]

Elvis Presley (1935–1977)

Singer

Memorable Film: *Viva Las Vegas* (1964).

Memorable Song: "Blue Suede Shoes" (1956).

Legendary rock n' roll pioneer Elvis Presley became bigger than life in the 1950s. The singer could not only sing, but also move his hips to the liking of millions of female fans. Presley also starred in many movies, including *Jailhouse Rock* (1957) and *Blue Hawaii* (1961). In 1977, Presley's heart gave-out and he died at the age of forty-two.

Elvis owned a home in Palm Springs in the 1970s.

Elvis Presley on images of stamps.

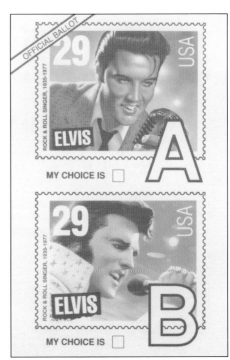

Home of Elvis Presley. [Value of card: $4-6.]

Home of Elvis Presley. [Value of card: $3-5.]

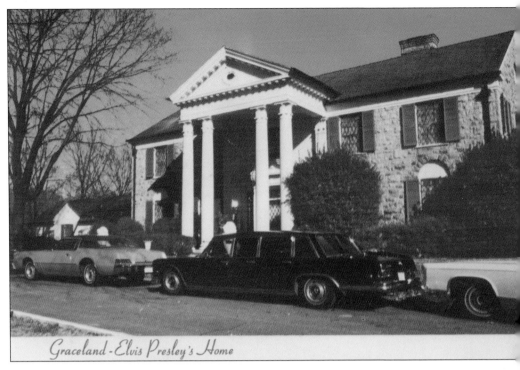

Home of Elvis Presley. [Value of card: $4-6.]

PRESLEY BIRTHPLACE

Elvis Presley Youth Center (not a home of Presley) and Presley birthplace (inset). [Value of card: $3-5.]

Aileen Pringle (1895–1989)

Actress

Memorable Films: *Three Weeks* (1924); *Body and Soul* (1927).

The daughter of a fruit company president, actress Aileen Pringle was a silent-film star. She made films for such studios as Famous Players-Lasky Corporation, Goldwyn Pictures Corporation, and MGM during the 1920s. Pringle became friends with Rudolph Valentino when the two appeared together in *Stolen Moments* (1920). Six years later, she was his date for the premiere of the acclaimed Valentino film, *Son of the Sheik* (1926). Pringle stayed active in movies until the early 1940s.

The Adelaide Place home, in Santa Monica, where Pringle once lived remains relatively unchanged by the years.

Aileen Pringle

Home of Aileen Pringle. [Value of card: $3-5.]

Esther Ralston (1902–1994)

Actress

Memorable Films: *Oliver Twist* (1922); *Children of Divorce* (1927).

The magazine *Film Weekly* put actress Esther Ralston on its September 30, 1932, cover. The blonde and gorgeous star made a fine cover picture. Ralston was a silent star who was awarded big roles in the mid-1920s.

Ralston lived in an impressive Hollyridge Drive home in the Hollywood Hills area of Los Angeles.

"Esther, my darling friend. I miss you terribly and think of you often. Those days on Hollyridge Drive were funfilled [*sic*] and memorable. Some of my fondest recollections are of you and George. Till we meet again my dearest friend. Love, Dottie"
—Actress Dorothy Dare

Esther Ralston

Esther Ralston

Home of Esther Ralston. [Value of card: $3-5.]

Home of Esther Ralston. [Value of card: $3-5.]

Charles Ray (1891–1943)

Actor

Memorable Films: *45 Minutes from Broadway* (1920); *The Old Swimmin' Hole* (1921).

Actor Charles Ray would appear in over 150 films. In many roles, he played a country boy with an innocent outlook on life. Ray would finance his own 1923 film called *The Courtship of Myles Standish*. It was a financial flop and brought ruin to Ray's personal finances.

Ray lived in a home on North Camden Drive in Beverly Hills.

Charles Ray

Home of Charles Ray.
[Value of card: $3-5.]

Donna Reed (1921–1986)

Actress

Memorable Film: *It's a Wonderful Life* (1946).

Memorable Television Show: "The Donna Reed Show" (1958–1966).

Actress Donna Reed started getting the public's attention early, winning a beauty queen title in high school. Playing Mary Hatch Bailey opposite James Stewart in *It's a Wonderful Life* (1946) immortalized her in the public's eye.

Home of Donna Reed.
[Value of card: $3-5.]

Wallace Reid (1891–1923)

Actor

Memorable Films: *The Birth of a Nation* (1915); *The Affairs of Anatol* (1921).

Wallace Reid was famous for acting in films and dying young, at age thirty-one. The popular silent star injured his back while filming *The Valley of the Giants* (1919). Reid was given morphine to ease his pain and would become hooked on it. He added to his troubles by drinking heavily. Reid soon started a descent into ever-declining health. Thousands attended his funeral in 1923.

Home of Wallace Reid. [Value of card: $3-5.]

Home of Wallace Reid. [Value of card: $4-6.]

128

Debbie Reynolds (1932–)

Actress

Memorable Films: *Singin' in the Rain* (1952); *The Unsinkable Molly Brown* (1964).

After winning a beauty contest in the late 1940s, actress Debbie Reynolds caught Hollywood's attention. She proved to be a quick study and became a star of many musicals of the 1950s. Reynolds has had her share of financial hard times. Her second husband, Harry Karl, was a gambler—and a bad one, at that.

Reynolds has a long history with Palm Springs, dating back to at least the mid-1950s. In the early 1960s, Reynolds moved to a Palm Springs home on East Racquet Club Road.

Debbie Reynolds

Home of Debbie Reynolds. [Value of card: $3-5.]

129

Irene Rich (1891–1988)

Actress

Memorable Films: *One Clear Call* (1922); *The Champ* (1931).

Born in New York, actress Irene Rich was a silent player who also appeared in sound pictures such as *The Champ* (1931), which starred Wallace Beery. By 1950, Rich's days in front of the camera were over.

Irene Rich

Irene Rich at home.
[Value of card: $3-5.]

Don Rickles (1926–)

Comedian/Actor

Memorable Films: *Run Silent, Run Deep* (1958); *Kelly's Heroes* (1970).

People who attend any show of stand-up comedian Don Rickles should come prepared to be on the receiving end of a jabbing joke or two. Trading comedic barbs with late-night legend Johnny Carson was fun for Rickles. "People said that whenever I went on the *Tonight* show, it was an event," Rickles recalled. "Johnny would get off his notes and shoot with both barrels. We had a ball."

Rickles has enjoyed calling Beverly Hills his home for many years.

Home of Don Rickles.
[From postcard packet.
Value of packet: $3-5.]

Charles "Buddy" Rogers (1904–1999)

Actor

Memorable Films: *Wings* (1927); *My Best Girl* (1927).

If he never married silent-star Mary Pickford, it is likely that actor Charles "Buddy" Rogers would be a long-forgotten Hollywood memory. Rogers married Pickford in 1937. He had a starring role in the 1927 movie, *Wings*. Rogers and Pickford adopted two children early in their marriage, but became estranged from them after the children grew up and moved away from Pickfair, their childhood home.

Rogers owned homes in Beverly Hills prior to marrying Pickford.

Charles "Buddy" Rogers

Home of Charles "Buddy" Rogers. [Value of card: $3-5.]

Charles "Buddy" Rogers at home. [From postcard packet. Value of packet: $3-5.]

Ginger Rogers (1911–1995)

Actress

Memorable Films: *Swing Time* (1936); *Kitty Foyle: The Natural History of a Woman* (1940).

Actress Ginger Rogers gained movie fame by dancing with Fred Astaire on film. The 1933 film, *Flying Down to Rio*, was the first film for the pair. In the early 1930s, before Rogers appeared in films with Astaire, he called her up for a date. Wondering what to wear, Rogers tried on two outfits before settling on a third. Rogers recalled Astaire showing up "very well dressed in a dark blue suit, starched white shirt, and burgundy silk tie."

In the late 1930s, Rogers built a home. Among its features were a projection room and a soda fountain. The home is located in what is called the Beverly Hills Post Office area. This area carries a Beverly Hills zip code, but actually falls outside city limits.

Ginger Rogers

"Performers are very fortunate. By virtue of our talents and recognition by the public through films and stage work, we have an entrée to people and places not accorded the average person."

—Ginger Rogers

Home of Ginger Rogers. [Value of card: $4-6.]

Home of Ginger Rogers. [Value of card: $8-10.]

Home of Ginger Rogers. [Value of card: $4-6.]

Will Rogers (1879–1935)

Actor

Memorable Films: *Doubling for Romeo* (1921); *State Fair* (1933).

Humorist and actor Will Rogers was raised around horses. He became a skilled rider and would learn to do trick roping. Rogers demonstrated his cowboy talents in the silent film, *The Ropin Fool* (1922). It was the first film Rogers would independently produce himself. Will Rogers Productions folded after just a few films, but he would recover and become a popular film star. Rogers's career suddenly ended when he was killed in a plane crash, in 1935.

Beverly Hills was still a young city when Rogers made it his home, circa 1920. Rogers once quipped, "I love to stroll down the old part of Beverly Hills, places that have been built for four or five years."

Will Rogers

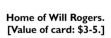

Home of Will Rogers.
[Value of card: $5-7.]

Home of Will Rogers.
[Value of card: $3-5.]

133

Home of Will Rogers. [From postcard packet. Value of packet: $3-5.]

Birthplace of Will Rogers. [Value of card: $3-5.]

Diana Ross (1944–)

Singer

Memorable Songs: "Ain't No Mountain High Enough" (1970); "Theme from Mahogany (Do You Know Where You're Going To?)" (1975).

Singer Diana Ross was born in a city that would hold her fate, Detroit, Michigan. Motown Record Corporation was also born in Detroit, and would launch Ross to stardom. She was part of the hit-making machine called The Supremes. "By the mid-1960s, life was becoming very difficult," Ross recalled. "We were basically living out of suitcases, touring endlessly, doing one-nighters all across the country, and recording albums, laced with touring

Home of Diana Ross. [From postcard packet. Value of packet: $3-5.]

through Europe." Ross left the group to perform and record as a solo artist.

Ross once lived on North Maple Drive in Beverly Hills.

Mme. Ernestine Schumann-Heink (1861–1936)

Singer

Memorable Performances: Carnegie Hall (1926); "Silent Night" sung over the radio each Christmas (1926–1935).

At one time, Austrian-born Mme. Ernestine Schumann-Heink was known as one of the world's greatest operatic contraltos. In 1899, she made her first appearance at the Metropolitan Opera in New York. After performing a concert at age sixty-four, Schumann-Heink told the press: "I am as happy as a child . . . Think of it! Singing almost fifty years before the public and still able to do my Erda, my Magdalena, and maybe my Fricka next winter. You

Mme. Ernestine Schumann-Heink at home. [Value of card: $5-7.]

know I am sixty-four years old and I learned a long time ago not to do more than I am able. And I am able to sing those roles again. Isn't it wonderful?"

In 1913, a seven-thousand dollar home in Grossmont, California, that Schumann-Heink had built was ready for occupancy. The home was on part of the five hundred acres of land the opera singer had purchased in 1910. She paid twenty thousand dollars for the property. In 1922, Schumann-Heink purchased the Coronado, California, home of John D. Spreckels.

Home of Mme. Ernestine Schumann-Heink. [Value of card: $5-7.]

William Seiter (1890–1964) and Laura La Plante (1904–1996)

Director (Seiter) and Actress (La Plante)

Memorable Films (William Seiter, as director): *Little Church Around the Corner* (1923); *Sons of the Desert* (1933).

Memorable Films (Laura La Plante): *Crooked Alley* (1923); *The Cat and the Canary* (1927).

William Seiter had a few acting jobs before launching his long directorial career in 1915 with a film called *The Honeymoon Roll*. The 1920s brought commercial success for the director. Seiter married actress Laura La Plante in the mid-1920s. La Plante would play in silent films with such stars as Tom Mix and Reginald Denny. The marriage of La Plante and Seiter ended in the mid-1930s.

Home of William Seiter and Laura La Plante. [Value of card: $5-7.]

Norma Shearer (1902–1983)

Actress

Memorable Films: *The Divorcee* (1930); *The Women* (1939).

Leading lady Norma Shearer not only starred in many MGM films, but in 1927, married one of its top executives, Irving Thalberg. The health of Thalberg was fragile, and he would die in 1936 at age thirty-seven. Shearer married again in 1942. Actor Douglas Fairbanks, Jr. knew Shearer and described her as "very pleasant indeed."

Norma Shearer

Home of Norma Shearer. [Value of card: $3-5.]

Dinah Shore (1916–1994)

Singer
Memorable Song: "Dear Hearts and Gentle People" (1949).
Memorable Television Show: "The Dinah Shore Show" (1951–1957).

Born in Tennessee, Dinah Shore recorded hit records and hosted her own television shows. She tried to make it in films in the 1940s, but her efforts did not take her far. Shore's television shows earned many Emmy Awards.

Dinah Shore

Home of Dinah Shore. [From postcard packet. Value of packet: $3-5.]

Dinah Shore (1916–1994) and George Montgomery (1916–2000)

Singer (Shore) and Actor (Montgomery)
Memorable Film (Dinah Shore): *Till the Clouds Roll By* (1946).
Memorable Television Show (Dinah Shore): "The Dinah Shore Show" (1951–1957).
Memorable Films (George Montgomery): *Cadet Girl* (1941); *Coney Island* (1943).

Dinah Shore worked with Frank Sinatra when both were amateur singers. As a professional singer, she had a hit record in the late 1940s called "Dear Hearts and Gentle People." The entertainer would host a number of television shows, including her own program, "Dinah's Place," which aired in the 1970s. Her romance with actor Burt Reynolds, who was much younger than Shore, generated a lot of Hollywood gossip in the 1970s. Years earlier, she had been married to the rugged-looking actor, George Montgomery. The couple married the same year Montgomery was starring in *Coney Island* (1943) and *Bomber's Moon* (1943). Shore and Montgomery divorced in 1963.

Home of Dinah Shore and George Montgomery. [Value of card: $3-5.]

Home of George Montgomery and wife Dinah Shore in Palm Springs

K5772

Milton Sills (1882–1930)

Actor

Memorable Films: *Flaming Youth* (1923); *The Sea Wolf* (1930).

Silent-star Milton Sills was born in Chicago, Illinois, in 1882. He attended the University of Chicago. Sills was married to actresses Gladys Wynne and Doris Kenyon. He died at forty-eight in Santa Barbara, California.

Milton Sills

MILTON SILLS.

Home of Milton Sills. [Value of card: $3-5.]

Simone Simon (1910–2005)

Actress

Memorable Films: *Seventh Heaven* (1937); *The Cat People* (1942).

French-born Simone Simon came to America to work in Hollywood in the mid-1930s. The actress had begun her film career in France. And, after making just a few films in the States it would be to France where she would return to make her famous movie, *La Bête Humaine* (1938). Simon never married during her long life.

North Maple Drive in Beverly Hills was home for Simon in the late 1930s.

Simone Simon

Home of Simone Simon. [Value of card: $10-12.]

Frank Sinatra (1915–1998)

Singer

Memorable Film: *From Here to Eternity* (1953).

Memorable Song: "My Way" (1968).

Frank Sinatra was a unique entertainer who captured the ears of the world with his vocal talents. The singer may have been known as "The Chairman of the Board," but Sinatra was a normal guy while at home in Rancho Mirage, California. Sinatra would "walk up and down the street just like everybody else," recalled his friend and former mayor of Palm Springs, Frank Bogert. "He never acted like a star. He was more of a native."

Sinatra purchased a Tamarisk Country Club home in Rancho Mirage in the mid-1950s. On Halloween night, Sinatra would pass out silver dollars to the trick-or-treating kids who stopped by the home.

HANDPRINT CEREMONY- GRAUMAN'S CHINESE THEATRE

Frank Sinatra at Grauman's Chinese Theater.

Home of Frank Sinatra. [Value of card: $3-5.]

Home of Frank Sinatra. [Value of card: $3-5.]

Red Skelton (1913–1997)

Comedian
Memorable Film: *Having a Wonderful Time* (1938).
Memorable Television Show: "The Red Skelton Show" (1951–1971).

    Raised in poverty by his mother, Red Skelton sang on the streets for money as a young child. The Indiana-born kid would not get many formal years of schooling. Skelton instead worked anywhere he could—including circuses and on vaudeville—to earn money. In the 1930s, he would become a radio success. Film and television followed, making Skelton a comedy star. He was known for playing comic characters such as Freddie the Freeloader.

Home of Red Skelton.
[Value of card: $3-5.]

Ann Sothern (1909–2001)

Actress
Memorable Films: *Trade Winds* (1938); *Letter to Three Wives* (1949).

    Uncredited appearances in films in the late 1920s launched Ann Sothern's movie career. The 1930s would take the actress from "B" films to first-rate feature films. The 1939 film, *Maisie,* was the turning point in Sothern's career. Beginning in the late 1950s, Sothern starred in the popular television program called "The Ann Sothern Show."

Home of Ann Sothern. [From postcard packet. Value of packet: $3-5.]

Barbara Stanwyck (1907–1990)

Actress

Memorable Films: *The Lady Eve* (1941); *Double Indemnity* (1944).

Actress Barbara Stanwyck became an orphan early in her childhood. This orphan would grow-up to be a stunning movie star who appeared in classic films such as *Double Indemnity* (1944). "Stanwyck doesn't act a scene, she *lives* it," said director Frank Capra, who worked with the actress.

Stanwyck lived in Beverly Hills and Westwood, an area of Los Angeles.

Home of Barbara Stanwyck. [From postcard packet. Value of packet: $3-5.]

Anita Stewart (1895–1961)

Actress

Memorable Films: *The Tale of Two Cities* (1911); *In Old Kentucky* (1919).

Born in New York, Anita Stewart began her acting career in films. Vitagraph Company of America put her to work in moving pictures, early in the silent-film era. The 1912 film, *The Godmother*, was among Stewart's first film appearances. The last feature film Stewart appeared in was released in the late 1920s.

Home of Anita Stewart. [From postcard packet. Value of packet: $3-5.]

James Stewart (1908–1997)

Actor

Memorable Films: *It's a Wonderful Life* (1946); *Vertigo* (1958).

Many classic films come to mind whenever actor James Stewart's name is mentioned. *Mr. Smith Goes to Washington* (1939), *It's a Wonderful Life* (1946), and *Broken Arrow* (1950) are just a few. He was strongest when he played men who had character and were steadfast in facing challenging odds.

Stewart was born and raised in Indiana, Pennsylvania. As an adult and star, he lived in Beverly Hills. Stewart was surprised when he learned that a nurse named Wilson, who took care of his small twin girls, was profiting from one of the sightseeing buses that stopped at his home. "One day I happened to come home early," he recalled, "and there was Wilson and a sightseeing bus, and everyone on it was peering out the window at the twins. Apparently, she had made a deal with the driver that if she'd tell the people how many times a day she had to change their diapers and what they ate and how much they slept, he'd give her some money."

RESIDENCE OF JAMES STEWART, BEVERLY HILLS, CALIFORNIA

Home of James Stewart. [From postcard packet. Value of packet: $3-5.]

Boyhood home of James Stewart. [Value of card: $3-5.]

Gloria Swanson (1897–1983)

Actress

Memorable Films: *The Trespasser* (1929); *Sunset Boulevard* (1950).

Gloria Swanson

She was a major silent-screen star, but Gloria Swanson is probably best remembered today for playing a faded star in *Sunset Boulevard* (1950). In the film, her character, Norma Desmond, believes she is still a huge star despite being decades past her prime. Desmond tells Joe Gillis, played by William Holden, that, "I am big, it's the pictures that got small!" Off-screen, Swanson was not so big, physically. Actor Tab Hunter met Swanson in the late-1950s at a dinner gathering. "I couldn't get over how tiny she was," Hunter remembered.

Swanson purchased a Palm Springs home in the 1970s. Much earlier in her life, while still a silent star, the actress had a so-called "dream palace" on North Crescent Drive in Beverly Hills.

Home of Gloria Swanson.
[Value of card: $4-6.]

Home of Gloria Swanson. [From postcard packet. Value of packet: $3-5.]

Blanche Sweet (1896–1986)

Actress

Memorable Films: *The Painted Lady* (1912); *Always Faithful* (1929).

Blanche Sweet is more than just an early silent-film star; she is a historic figure of the screen. Legendary director D.W. Griffith would make the actress his first leading lady. Some have called Sweet "Hollywood's first-leading lady."

Sweet owned a North Camden Drive house in Beverly Hills before leaving films in the 1930s.

Blanche Sweet

Home of Blanche Sweet. [From postcard packet. Value of packet: $3-5.]

Norma Talmadge (1893–1957)

Actress

Memorable Films: *Smilin' Through* (1922); *Camille* (1927).

Actress Norma Talmadge entered films as a teenager. Natalie Talmadge, who married Buster Keaton, and actress Constance Talmadge, were her sisters. Screenwriter Frederica Sagor Maas spent time in the mid-1920s in Coronado, California, with Talmadge and her first husband, producer Joe Schenck. Maas recalled, "Joe Schenck and Norma Talmadge—what an odd couple they were. In the two weeks we spent together, they rarely spoke or even looked at each other." After divorcing Schenck in the mid-1930s, Talmadge would marry another producer, George Jessel.

Home of Norma Talmadge. [Value of card: $3-5.]

Home of Norma Talmadge. [Value of card: $3-5.]

Estelle Taylor (1894–1958) and Jack Dempsey (1895–1983)

Actress (Taylor) and Boxer/Actor (Dempsey)
Memorable Films (Estelle Taylor): *Dorothy Vernon of Haden Hall* (1924); *Cimarron* (1931).
Memorable Films (Jack Dempsey): *Daredevil Jack* (1920); *Manhattan Madness* (1925).

Born in Delaware, Estelle Taylor made it to stardom in the silent-film era. She had brown hair and brown eyes and would work for studios such as Vitagraph Company of America and Fox Film Corporation. After the 1920s, Taylor's movie work was less frequent. Boxer Jack Dempsey began picking up film-work in the 1920s, including some short-films for Universal Pictures. Taylor and Dempsey became a married couple in the mid-1920s. Their union did not last past 1930.

Estelle Taylor

ESTELLE TAYLOR AND JACK DEMPSEY AT THEIR BEAUTIFUL HOME IN LAUGHLIN PARK, HOLLYWOOD

Estelle Taylor and Jack Dempsey at home. [From postcard packet. Value of packet: $3-5.]

Robert Taylor (1911–1969)

Actor

Memorable Films: *Johnny Eager* (1942); *Quo Vadis* (1951).

    The handsome, blue-eyed actor Robert Taylor milked the Hollywood studio system during his career. Beginning in the 1930s, he would work for MGM for over two decades. When directors got Taylor, they got a hard-working actor. Taylor was married to actress Barbara Stanwyck for over a decade starting in the late 1930s.

Robert Taylor

Home of Robert Taylor. [Value of card: $3-5.]

Shirley Temple (1928–)

Actress

Memorable Films: *Bright Eyes* (1934); *Since You Went Away* (1944).

There is a reason why it is hard to picture Shirley Temple as anything other than a kid who is perky and oh-so cute. The actress was only twenty-one years old when her last picture was released in 1949. Temple starred in *Curly Top* (1935) and many other films in the 1930s and 1940s. She married the late Charles Black in 1960 and has since gone by the name of Shirley Temple Black.

Shirley Temple

Home of Shirley Temple. [Value of card: $5-7.]

Spencer Tracy (1900–1967)

Actor

Memorable Films: *Boy's Town* (1938); *Guess Who's Coming to Dinner* (1967).

Actor Spencer Tracy made many classic films. Producer Leland Hayward bought the movie rights to Ernest Hemingway's tale *The Old Man and the Sea* and sought out Tracy for the lead role. According to socialite Slim Keith, Hayward's wife at the time, Tracy initially resisted getting involved with the film. Keith said, "Spencer thought it was the most ridiculous idea to make a movie about a fish—and judging by the way that film turned out, Spence was right." Besides movies, Tracy is famous for a years-long romance with actress Katharine Hepburn while he remained married to his only wife, Louise.

In the mid-1930s, Tracy bought a ranch in the Encino area of Los Angeles where he would live for nearly two decades.

Spencer Tracy

Home of Spencer Tracy. [Value of card: $3-5.]

Ben Turpin (1869–1940)

Actor

Memorable Films: *The Small Town Idol* (1921); *The Daredevil* (1923).

Ben Turpin built an acting career around of his famous crossed eyes. He did a lot of work for the man famous for producing the Keystone Kops comedy-films of the silent era, Mack Sennett. Turpin appeared in *The Battle Royal* (1918) and *The Star Boarder* (1920) under Sennett's employ. He devoted time in caring for his wife when she took ill in the mid-1920s. "What's the good of all the money I got if it can't make my wife well?" Turpin told the press several months before his wife died, in 1925.

Turpin moved to a house on North Canon Drive in Beverly Hills in the 1920s.

Ben Turpin

RESIDENCE OF BEN TURPIN, BEVERLY HILLS, CALIFORNIA

Home of Ben Turpin. [Value of card: $5-7.]

Helen Twelvetrees (1908–1958)

Actress

Memorable Films: *Painted Desert* (1931); *State's Attorney* (1932).

The film career of Helen Twelvetrees would last about a decade and be confined almost exclusively to the 1930s. She managed to work with some big names of Hollywood, such as Clark Gable and John Barrymore. Twelvetrees would die suddenly in 1958 at the age of forty-nine. At the time, she had been living in Harrisburg, Pennsylvania, with her husband. The petite Twelvetrees had long before exited Hollywood. The Dauphin County Coroner called her death a suicide.

The Hollywood Hills home where Twelvetrees once lived remains relatively unchanged, despite decades passing since the actress left it.

829   HOME OF HELEN TWELVETREES, BRENTWOOD HEIGHTS, CALIFORNIA

Home of Helen Twelvetrees. [Value of card: $5-7.]

Conway Twitty (1933–1993)

Singer

Memorable Songs: "After the Fire Is Gone" (1971); "As Soon as I Hang Up the Phone" (1974).

Country singer Conway Twitty had over fifty hit records in his career. His most famous song was "Hello Darlin'," released in 1970.

Twitty had a famous estate in Hendersonville, Tennessee. The home was part of Twitty City, an entertainment complex that opened in 1982. But Twitty did not let the public inside the mansion until 1991. Twitty City would include gardens and waterfalls. The tourist destination is no longer in operation.

Conway Twitty at home. [Value of card: $3-5.]

Rudolph Valentino (1895–1926)

Actor

Memorable Films: *The Sheik* (1921); *The Four Horsemen of the Apocalypse* (1921).

The name Rudolph Valentino conjures up an image of the ultimate romantic male. Today, Valentino is arguably the best-known silent-era leading man. He was gutsy in his pursuit of a movie career. Valentino once walked up to actress Mary Pickford in a restaurant and asked for her "advice as to how I may get into motion pictures." He hit stardom in the early 1920s. Silent star and party girl Gertrude Astor invited friend Valentino to parties at her Hollywood mansion in the early 1920s. "He was very charming and good looking, and very damned sexy," she recalled. "I can vouch for that." Valentino's career was cut short by his death in 1926 at age thirty-one.

In late 1921, Valentino bought a mansion in the Whitley Heights area of Los Angeles. The home, on Wedgewood Place, was not in good shape when he moved his belongings into the house. It was without power and heat at the time.

Rudolph Valentino mounted on Jadaan, a horse used in the film *The Son of the Sheik* (1926).

Home of Rudolph Valentino. [Value of card: $3-5.]

Florence Vidor (1895–1977)

Actress

Memorable Films: *The Countess Charming* (1917); *Alice Adams* (1923).

Florence Vidor was a silent star who worked for a few of Hollywood's early studios. The actress did a film called *The Yellow Girl* in 1916 for Vitagraph Company of America. Vidor starred in *The Widow's Might* in 1918 for Jesse Lasky Feature Play Company. Director King Vidor became her husband in 1915. They would divorce in the 1920s.

Florence Vidor

Florence Vidor

Home of Florence Vidor. [Value of card: $3-5.]

Robert Wagner (1930–)

Actor

Memorable Television Shows: "It Takes a Thief" (1968–1970); "Hart to Hart" (1979–1983).

Suave Robert Wagner became a star in the early 1950s. Hollywood took notice when the actor had a scene-stealing role as a soldier in *With a Song in My Heart* (1952).

He has connected with today's young audiences with his role of Number Two in the *Austin Powers* movies. Wagner is famous for marrying actress Natalie Wood twice.

Home of Robert Wagner. [Value of card: $3-5.]

Henry Walthall (1878–1936)

Actor

Memorable Films: *The Birth of a Nation* (1915); *Judge Priest* (1934).

Henry Walthall played Colonel Ben Cameron, a.k.a. "the little colonel" in the controversial silent film, *The Birth of a Nation* (1915). He appeared in the film with legendary actress Lillian Gish. The two did many films together. He died in 1936 at Pasteur Sanitarium in Monrovia, California.

Walthall began living on North Beverly Drive in Beverly Hills during the mid-1920s.

**Home of Henry Walthall.
[Value of card: $3-5.]**

Bryant Washburn (1889–1963)

Actor

Memorable Films: *Till I Come Back to You* (1918); *Temptation* (1923).

Actor Bryant Washburn starred in such films as *Try and Get It* (1924) and *Young April* (1926). A 1928 article in the *New York Times* told of actress Mabel Forrest divorcing Washburn. The article stated that Forrest had claimed Washburn had been "cruel and indifferent" towards her during their marriage. In 1929, Washburn would marry actress Virginia Vance.

Home of Bryant Washburn. [Value of card: $3-5.]

Lawrence Welk (1903–1992)

Musician

Memorable Television Show: "The Lawrence Welk Show" (1955–1982).

Lawrence Welk brought accordion-playing and plenty of bubbles into the living rooms of millions of viewers during the twenty-seven year run of his television show, "The Lawrence Welk Show." Early in his career, Welk sold his car in order to force himself to walk. His goal was to lose the extra pounds he had recently put on. In combination with a strict diet, Welk claimed this "drastic cure" was successful.

"A showman named George T. Kelly tried to make an actor out of me way back in the twenties. After a few frustrating months, he gave up completely and solved the problem by casting me as the corpse in the murder-mystery plays we presented."

—Lawrence Welk

Home of Lawrence Welk. [Value of card: $3-5.]

Lois Wilson (1894–1988)

Actress

Memorable Films: *Monsieur Beaucaire* (1924); *The Great Gatsby* (1926).

By the time she retired from the screen, Lois Wilson had acted in over one-hundred films. She played opposite leading man J. Warren Kerrigan in the 1923 film, *The Covered Wagon*. Wilson recalled that the "conditions were rough" during its filming. "I got slight frostbite, we ran out of supplies and had to live on apples and baked beans for a while," she remembered, "but I loved ever minute of *The Covered Wagon*."

Home of Lois Wilson. [From postcard packet. Value of packet: $3-5.]

Jane Withers (1926–)

Actress

Memorable Films: *Bright Eyes* (1934); *Giant* (1956).

Jane Withers caught the wave of the public's demand for child stars in the hardship-times of the 1930s. In 1934, the actress was cast in the Shirley Temple film, *Bright Eyes* and was on her way to stardom. The 1960s brought the actress new fame on television as Josephine the Plumber in Comet cleaner commercials.

Home of Jane Withers. [Value of card: $3-5.]

Robert Young (1907–1998)

Actor

Memorable Television Shows: "Father Knows Best" (1954–1960); "Marcus Welby, M.D." (1969–1976).

Actor Robert Young's television success overshadowed a film career that took off in the 1930s. *The Kid from Spain* (1932) and *Tugboat Annie* (1933) were among the first handful of films he made in his long acting career. In the mid-1950s, Young began his work on television's "Father Knows Best" series. It would end in the 1960s. In the late 1960s, Young began "Marcus Welby," another successful television series.

Young had a home in Beverly Hills on North Elm Drive.

Home of Robert Young. [From postcard packet. Value of packet: $3-5.]

Darryl F. Zanuck (1902–1979)

Producer

Memorable Films (as producer): *How Green Was My Valley* (1941); *Twelve O'Clock High* (1949).

Darryl Zanuck was a movie mogul during and after the era of the Hollywood studio system. During his early twenties, he wrote comedy for silent-film legend Charles Chaplin. Apparently, the two never clicked. Zanuck declared Chaplin to be "nothing but a show-off." Upon being introduced to Chaplin, Zanuck recalled that, "Charlie took an instant dislike to me." French director Jean Renoir, who worked with Zanuck in the early 1940s, described him in a 1960 interview: "He's not only a boss who sits down in an office; he's a man who knows perfectly what's going on in the cutting room and is himself a very good cutter."

In 1943, Zanuck bought an estate on East Tamarisk Road in Palm Springs. He owned it until his death, in 1979. Over the years, visitors to the mansion would include actors Douglas Fairbanks, Jr., Jennifer Jones, Tyrone Power, and Judy Garland.

Home of Darryl F. Zanuck. [Value of card: $3-5.]

Selected Bibliography

Fox, Charles Donald and Milton L. Silver. *Who's Who on the Screen*. New York City: Ross Publishing Co., 1920. Reprint, New York: Gordon Press, 1976.

Internet Movie Database, Inc. http://www.imdb.com.

Johns, Howard. *Palm Springs Confidential: Playground of the Stars*. Fort Lee, New Jersey: Barricade, 2004.

Monush, Barry. *The Encyclopedia of Hollywood Film Actors: From the Silent Era to 1965*. New York, New York: Applause Theatre & Cinema Books, 2003.

Slide, Anthony. *Silent Players: A Biographical and Autobiographical Study of 100 silent-film Actors and Actresses*. Lexington, Kentucky: The University Press of Kentucky, 2002.